W9-BNT-687

Georgia

GEORGIA BY ROAD

NATIONAL FOREST

URBAN AREA

0 10 20 30 40 50 60 70 80

MILES

Brasstown Bald
(4,784 ft.)

Chattahoochee National Forest

Dalton

Chattahoochee
National
Forest

Toccoa

Lake
Sidney
Lanier

Coosa R.

Rome

Gainesville

Roswell

Marietta

Athens

Atlanta

Newnan

Jackson
Lake

Oconee

Augusta

Lake
Oconee

Waynesboro

West
Point
Lake

Griffin

National

Forest

Milledgeville

La Grange

Macon

Warner Robins

Swainsboro

Columbus

Dublin

Statesboro

Vidalia

Americus

Cordele

Savannah

Lake
Blackshear

Walter
George
Reservoir

Albany

Douglas

Jesup

Moultrie

Waycross

Brunswick

Bainbridge

Thomasville

Valdosta

Lake
Seminole

Chattahoochee R.

Flint R.

Ocmulgee R.

Oconee R.

Ogeechee R.

Savannah R.

Altamaha R.

Alapaha R.

Little R.

Suwannee R.

St. Mary's R.

Oconee R.

ATLANTIC OCEAN

N
W   E
S

Celebrate the States

Georgia

Steve Otfinoski

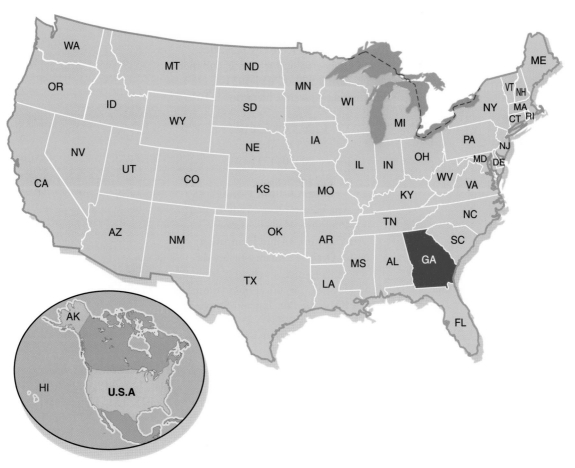

mc Marshall Cavendish
Benchmark

New York

To the Corriere and Nelson families, who dearly love their home state

Marshall Cavendish Benchmark
99 White Plains Road
Tarrytown, NY 10591-5502
www.marshallcavendish.us

All Internet addresses were correct and accurate at the time of printing.

Library of Congress Cataloging-in-Publication Data
Otfinoski, Steven.
Georgia / by Steve Otfinoski.—2nd ed.
p. cm. — (Celebrate the states)
Summary: "Provides comprehensive information on the geography, history, wildlife, governmental
structure, economy, cultural diversity, peoples, religion, and landmarks of
Georgia"—Provided by publisher.
Includes bibliographical references and index.
ISBN 978-0-7614-4031-4
1. Georgia—Juvenile literature. I. Title.

F286.3.O84 2010
975.8—dc22
2008041711

Editor: Christine Florie
Co-Editor: Denise Pangia
Publisher: Michelle Bisson
Art Director: Anahid Hamparian
Series Designer: Adam Mietlowski

Photo research and layout by Marshall Cavendish International (Asia) Private Limited—
Thomas Khoo, Benson Tan and Shawn Wee

Cover photo by Photolibrary

The photographs in this book are used by permission and through the courtesy of, *Getty Images*:
back cover, 15, 43, 55, 56, 57, 64, 66, 73, 79, 111, 112, 113, 115, 116, 117, 119, 121, 123,
124, 127; *Corbis*: 8, 13, 14, 36, 39, 41, 50, 68, 72, 75, 82, 84, 120, 125, 131, 133, 135;
Photolibrary: 10, 16, 17, 19, 20, 22, 25, 26, 29, 30, 31, 33, 44, 59, 61, 62, 70, 74, 77, 83, 86,
94, 95, 99, 102, 103, 106, 108; *North Wind Picture Archives*: 24; *Photolibrary / Alamy*: 28, 47,
90, 92, 109, 128 129, 130, 136; *Reuters*: 89.

Printed in Malaysia
1 3 5 6 4 2

Contents

Georgia Is . . .

Georgia is a state of contrasts . . .

"Here is a land where modern fortresses [Air Force bases] are not far from communities where sacred harp singing is still carried on . . . a land of forested mountains, deep lakes, and clear mountain streams, contrasted with miles of sunny beaches and sun-drenched isles, with still further contrast in the misty swamps where alligators splash and exotic tropical birds preen their elaborate plumage."

—former Georgia governor and U.S. president Jimmy Carter

. . . and more than a few surprises.

"My version of 'Georgia [on My Mind]' became the state song of Georgia. That was a big thing for me, man. It really touched me. Here is a state that used to lynch people like me suddenly declaring my version of a song as its state song. That is touching."

—Ray Charles, musician and singer

It is a state of great natural beauty . . .

"To me the best symbol for Georgia is the pine tree, which flourishes in our region of the state. Tall and straight, it reaches upward to the endless possibility of the sky. And yet it needs its roots to be thrust deep into the red clay soil from which it gets its sustenance. It is always green and thriving, providing a haven for birds and beasts of the forest as well as useful products for mankind."

—Carol C. Nelson, homemaker

. . . cultural riches . . .

"As a college student in Atlanta in the 1950s and early 60s, I was swept away by the dazzling array of Atlanta attractions—the High Museum, jazz at the Wits' End, traveling companies of Broadway road shows, classy restaurants, the

Cyclorama, Piedmont Park, art-house movie theaters, the Zoo, the Fox Theatre with its sparkling night-sky ceiling, the Atlanta library, the glitter of Five Points. Returning to work in Atlanta in the 1990s, it was amazing how much from my college days was still there, but kicked up many, many more notches."

—Dr. Anthony Paredes, former regional ethnographer
for the Southeast region of the National Park Service

. . . and warm, friendly people.

"The state of Georgia's greatest asset is its people. They're good people with good hearts. When I was ill some years ago, I got a lot of help from unexpected places. People reached out and helped me in many ways. My Catholic church participates in a soup kitchen at a local rescue mission here in Macon. Several other churches participate, including Protestant churches and a Jewish temple. When people are in need, everyone puts aside their political and religious differences to help."

—Leonard Corriere, dispatcher for a trucking company

Is it any wonder that people love living in Georgia?

"I couldn't imagine living anywhere else but Georgia. We have the mountains of the Appalachian Trail and the beaches within a few hours' reach. Although our public elementary school has doubled in size since my oldest child began there in 1997, it has a small neighborhood atmosphere that my 'baby' (second grader) still enjoys. (And we are still walking to school eleven years later!)"

—Liz Lane Portwood, homemaker

Georgia is a place, whether to live or just visit, that people never forget. There is something about its magical land and gracious people that inspires songwriters and visitors alike. "Georgia on My Mind" is just one of the many songs that have been written about this beautiful southern state. It truly stays "on the mind" of anyone who has visited it.

Chapter One

Empire State of the South

Georgia is often called the Empire State of the South. And for good reason. It is not only the largest state east of the Mississippi River but it also has one of the East's largest economies. If Georgia were a country by itself, it would have the twenty-eighth largest economy in the world. Georgia lies in the heart of the South and has a big heart. The warmth of its people is matched only by the natural beauty of its land.

FROM THE MOUNTAINS TO THE SEA

Georgia is bordered on the north by Tennessee and North Carolina and on the east by South Carolina. Its neighbor to the south is Florida, and to the west, Alabama. The state can be divided into three major regions: mountains in the north, a fertile plateau in the center, and an enormous plain that blankets the southern half of the state.

Two important mountain chains in northern Georgia are the Cumberland Plateau and the Blue Ridge Mountains. These are among the most scenic and accessible mountains in the eastern United States.

A view of Amicalola State Park can be seen from atop Amicalola Falls, the highest waterfall east of the Mississippi River.

The 2,175-mile-long (3,500-kilometer-long) Appalachian Trail, a magnet for hikers, ends at Georgia's Springer Mountain. "Hikers starting out here on the Appalachian Trail find it cruel and unusual punishment," says photographer George Whiteley of Atlanta. "From Amicalola Falls State

The Appalachian Trail offers many opportunities to explore, experience, and connect with nature.

Park to Springer Mountain is straight up." Whiteley's favorite stopping place along the trail is Blood Mountain, one of Georgia's highest peaks. "It was named after a legendary battle between two Cherokee tribes," he explains. "The legend says the warriors' blood ran down the mountain trail." The Chattahoochee-Oconee National Forest, which primarily consists of the Blue Ridge Mountains, contains Brasstown Bald, Georgia's highest mountain, and Lake Consauga, its highest body of water.

To the south is the Piedmont, which has rich red soil and rolling hills. It is the most developed and populated part of the state. Peaches, soybeans, and tobacco are among the many crops Piedmont farmers grow.

Georgia's many rivers flow into the Atlantic Ocean or the Gulf of Mexico. Some have colorful names, such as Chattahoochee, Ogeechee, Ohoopee, and Ochlockonee—reminders of Georgia's rich American Indian heritage. Georgia's best-known river is often recognized by the wrong name. Composer Stephen Foster wrote his famous song "Swanee River" about the gentle Suwannee River that runs through Okefenokee Swamp. If Foster misspelled it, maybe it was because he had never seen it, nor even been in Georgia.

Okefenokee Swamp is tucked into the southeastern corner of the state and extends into Florida. The second-largest freshwater swamp in the United States, it abounds with plant and animal life.

The swamp remains a wildlife preserve, but much of the rest of the coastal plain that covers southern Georgia has been turned into farmland. Its sandy soil is perfect for growing such crops as peanuts. Georgia grows more peanuts, which southerners call goobers, than any other state. This accounts for another of its nicknames, the Goober State.

LAND AND WATER

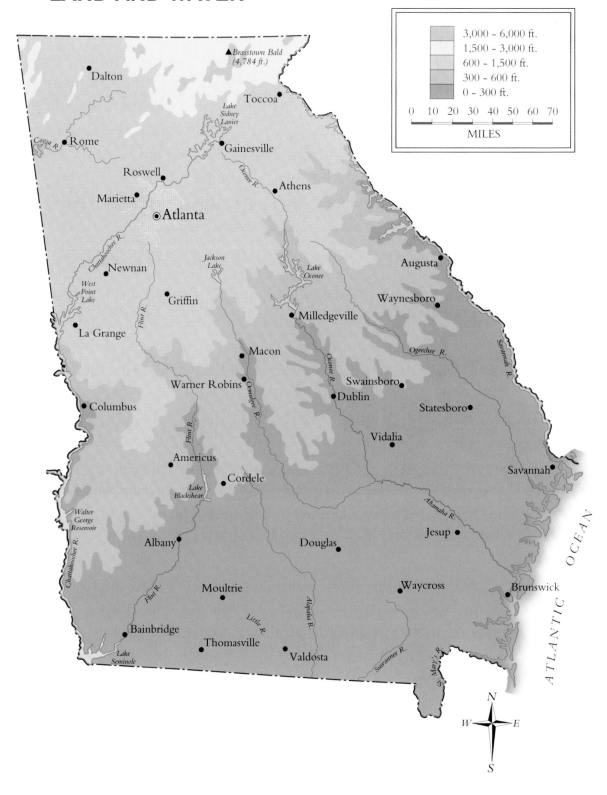

▲ *Brasstown Bald (4,784 ft.)*

	3,000 – 6,000 ft.
	1,500 – 3,000 ft.
	600 – 1,500 ft.
	300 – 600 ft.
	0 – 300 ft.

0 10 20 30 40 50 60 70
MILES

Dalton

Toccoa

Lake Sidney Lanier

Coosa R. Rome

Gainesville

Roswell

Oconee R. Athens

Marietta

◉ Atlanta

Chattahoochee R. Newnan

Jackson Lake

Lake Oconee

Augusta

West Point Lake

Griffin

Waynesboro

Flint R.

La Grange

Milledgeville

Macon

Ogeechee R.

Savannah R.

Warner Robins

Ocmulgee R.

Oconee R.

Swainsboro

Dublin

Columbus

Statesboro

Flint R.

Vidalia

Americus

Savannah

Cordele

Lake Blackshear

Altamaha R.

Walter George Reservoir

Jesup

Chattahoochee R.

Albany

Douglas

Moultrie

Waycross

Brunswick

Bainbridge

Flint R.

Little R.

Alapaha R.

Thomasville

Valdosta

Suwannee R.

St. Marys R.

Lake Seminole

ATLANTIC OCEAN

N
W   E
S

OKEFENOKEE SWAMP

The Indians called it Owauquaphenoga, which means "trembling earth." The description is fitting. Much of Okefenokee Swamp is made up of floating islands composed of peat moss. If you stamp on the ground, the trees and plants shake.

But there is nothing impermanent about Georgia's largest swamp. It is a refuge for thousands of birds, animals, and fish. The Seminole and Creek Indians once hunted bears, otters, and alligators there; these animals are now protected in the Okefenokee National Wildlife Refuge, established in 1937. The refuge encompasses much of the 684-square-mile (1,772-square-km) swamp.

Because a lot of the swamp is remote and uninhabited, and its old trees and dark water make it seem mysterious, many stories have arisen about it, some going back to the time before Europeans settled in the area. Encounters with ghosts, the legendary creature known as Bigfoot, and even UFOs have been reported in Okefenokee. No one, however, has sighted the most famous "residents" of the swamp, cartoonist Walt Kelly's comic-strip characters Pogo the possum and his friends.

Georgia's 100-mile (161-km) coast along the Atlantic Ocean is deceptively small. If you were to straighten out all its bays and river mouths and include its offshore islands, the coastline would measure 2,344 miles (3,772 km)!

The jewels of Georgia's coast are the Golden Isles. They include Jekyll, Sea, Saint Simons, and Tybee islands. While all four lure tourists from near and far, each has its own special attractions. Jekyll Island is a park where visitors can enjoy a wildlife refuge and miles of untouched sandy beaches. Sea Island features a trendy resort for enjoying a secluded vacation, while Saint Simons houses the ruins of Fort Frederica, built by Georgia's founding father, James Oglethorpe. Tybee Island, the most visited of the Golden Isles, has some of the best public beaches.

Fort Frederica National Monument, on Saint Simons Island, preserves the archaeological remnants of a fort and town built by James Oglethorpe between 1736 and 1748.

HOT AND MILD

Most of Georgia has mild winters and hot, humid summers, although cooling summer rains can make the heat more bearable. "I like Georgia in the fall, winter, and spring," says Sue Strickland, who lives in Atlanta. "I don't like Georgia in the summer. It's hot and humid. Then there's the poison ivy and the mosquitoes. They limit my yardwork."

The tornadoes that swept through Atlanta in March 2008 damaged a number of city landmarks.

Beginning in 2007 and continuing into 2009, Georgia and the rest of the South experienced the worst drought in a century. State and local officials put severe restrictions on water use. Residents were even encouraged to save bathwater to water their plants.

The state averages only 1.5 inches (3.81 centimeters) of snow a year, usually in the higher elevations. When the odd winter storm strikes the state, traffic is often paralyzed because motorists aren't used to driving in snow and ice. Hurricanes have occasionally swept across Georgia's coastline, but it has been spared much of the devastation that has struck the coasts of Florida and the Carolinas. Tornadoes are infrequent visitors but can hit hard, as they did in March 2008, striking downtown Atlanta with such destructive force that the mayor declared a state of emergency.

WILD THINGS

The live oak is the state tree of Georgia. The resilience of this majestic tree, which is often festooned with Spanish moss, symbolizes the state's hardy and varied wildlife.

The elderberry tree not only produces lovely flowers but also berries that provide food for many birds.

Nearly three-quarters of the state is covered by forest. The sweet-scented pine is the state's most prevalent tree, found in forests in both the north and south. In spring the woods are alive with gorgeous flowering trees, such as magnolia, dogwood, and elderberry. Fires caused by downed wires and lightning swept across Okefenokee Swamp and the region surrounding it in the spring of 2007, burning more than half a million acres (202,343 hectares), much of it forestland. It was the worst forest fire in the state in fifty years.

Each region of the state has its own cherished plants. Laurels and flowering rhododendron dot the misty mountains. The coastal region is alive with such colorful wildflowers as Japanese honeysuckle and the white-blossomed Cherokee rose, the state flower. Tall salt grass and cattails bend gracefully in the gentle breezes passing over salt marshes and swamps.

More than nine hundred species of wild animals and birds live in Georgia. Black bears, deer, foxes, and opossums roam the northern mountains, while rivers and swamps abound with muskrats, wild boars, alligators, and a host of snakes, some of them poisonous, such as the coral snake, copperhead, and water moccasin. Birds of every description make their home in such protected refuges as Cumberland Island and Okefenokee Swamp.

Among the poisonous snakes of North America, only the venom of certain rattlesnakes is more deadly than that of this coral snake.

A BATTLE FOR WATER

For years Georgia's man-made Lake Lanier has been the main source of water for metropolitan Atlanta, the state capital, a region with a population of five million. As the lake's water level dropped perilously low during the long drought of 2007–2009, state officials lobbied for the U.S. Army Corps of Engineers to reduce the flow of water from Lanier southward to rivers in Alabama and Florida. This caused water problems in these two neighboring states. Especially hard hit was the $10 million oyster industry in Florida's Apalachicola Bay. The oysters need a balance of freshwater and saltwater to thrive in the bay, and the reduction of freshwater from Lanier was killing off many oyster beds.

It was a case of "man vs. mussels," according to Georgia governor Sonny Perdue. Like many Georgians, he saw the needs of humans outweighing those of mollusks. But the oyster workers of Florida disagreed. "People in Atlanta need water and they need it to survive, but we do too," said oyster worker Carolyn Syzdek. "This is our home." The battle over water between Georgia, Alabama, and Florida moved into the courts in 2008. Whatever the final settlement is, it may come too late to save the livelihoods of northwest Florida's oyster workers.

MUSSELS IN TROUBLE

Oysters are not the only mollusks that Georgians have placed in danger. In their own state several species of mussels are threatened. These small, elongated freshwater mollusks live in creeks, streams, and small rivers that have been polluted by industry. The cutting down of nearby forests has caused the waterways to dry up, robbing the mussels of their habitat.

Zebra mussels, which are native to Russia, first appeared in American waterways in 1988. Since then, they have disturbed the ecological balance not only in Georgia, but many other states.

The colorfully named shinyrayed pocketbook is a mussel with another problem. The zebra mussel, which is not native to Georgia but was introduced accidentally some years ago, has taken over much of the food and space that the shinyrayed pocketbook rely on.

The fat three-ridge mussel may already be a memory in Georgia, as it is now believed to be found only in Florida. Specimens of this mussel were last seen in Georgia's Apalachicola River in 1996. It is now protected by state and federal laws.

At least this mussel has a chance of survival. The southern acornshell, another native mussel, was last seen in 1974. Most experts believe it is extinct. Unless more is done to protect these tiny mollusks' remaining habitat, many of them may follow the southern acornshell into extinction.

GROWING AND SPRAWLING

For several decades Atlanta has welcomed newcomers from rural areas and other states with open arms. This influx of new residents has strengthened the state's economy and given the capital a modern, cosmopolitan atmosphere not found elsewhere in the South.

Between 2000 and 2006 Atlanta was the fastest-growing metropolitan area in the United States, as seen from this magnificent skyline.

But this growth has come at a price. In 2007 Atlanta was the nation's ninth-largest metropolitan area. It encompasses ten counties with a population of just over five million. From 2000 to 2006 the metropolitan population grew by about 20 percent, making it the fastest-growing metropolitan area in the nation. The city's suburban sprawl has created the longest commute for workers in any city in the country—36.5 daily miles (58.7 km) round trip on average, 16 miles (26 km) farther than the average in Los Angeles, California.

And the city continues to sprawl. Every day more than 50 acres (20 ha) of green space in greater Atlanta are destroyed for new development. Once-rustic neighborhoods are now surrounded by shopping malls and commercial strips. "People who visited us five years ago say, 'I couldn't find your house,'" complains Julie Haley of Alpharetta. "The roads have all gotten wider, they've knocked down all the trees, there's a million shopping centers."

The state government is doing what it can to stop or at least slow the sprawl and improve residents' quality of life. Former governor Roy Barnes created a new agency called the Georgia Regional Transportation Authority in April 1999 to extend the city's mass transit system to the suburbs and therefore reduce the number of people commuting in cars, a major source of air pollution. "This whole process in regard to regional transportation has been to make sure we continued to grow and not stop it," Governor Barnes stressed. "But it has to be growth in a planned sort of way."

Finding a way for Georgia to grow while still meeting the needs of both urban and suburban dwellers is a major issue facing the state today.

Chapter Two

Georgia in the Making

Over its long history Georgia has meant many things to many people. Spanish explorers called conquistadores saw it as a fabled land full of gold. British colony builders saw it as a home for Britain's poor and needy. Later, wealthy farmers saw it as a promised land of prosperity and easy living. The African-American slaves who worked their plantations had a very different opinion of the state. Through good times and bad Georgians have shown a remarkable ability to rise above their troubles, to reinvent themselves, and to create triumph from tragedy.

GEORGIA'S FIRST PEOPLE

About 11,000 years ago the first inhabitants of present-day Georgia hunted large animals. As time went on, they settled in villages and grew plants for food. They made pottery, the first in North America, by about 2500 B.C.E. By about 1000 C.E. the people living in what is now Georgia were building large ceremonial centers with earthen mounds, some as high as 60 feet (18 meters). They were part of a civilization called the Mound Builders. Experts believe these mounds were gathering places

Hard-working prospectors searched for gold near Dahlonega in northwestern Georgia, the site of America's first gold rush beginning in 1828.

that played a central role in the Mound Builders' religious and political life.

The Cherokee, whose name in the Choctaw language means "those who live in the cave country," came from the north. The Creek, so named by English settlers because they often settled alongside streams, came from the southeast.

Both the Creek and Cherokee were skillful farmers and hunters. They raised corn, squash, beans, and pumpkins. In the forests they hunted deer and bear, and they caught fish and turtle in the streams and rivers. The Creek were the most numerous tribe. Some of the fifty Creek towns in the area had populations of one thousand. Each town had a plaza

Corn and maize were principal crops for the Creek and Cherokee of Georgia.

used for religious ceremonies and games. Houses with roofs made of wood shingles or grass surrounded the plaza. Although they were living in different regions, the Creek and Cherokee clashed over land boundaries. These disputes were sometimes settled peacefully by a ball game rather than through warfare.

CONQUISTADORES AND PIRATES

The Indians' first encounters with European explorers were not pleasant. Spanish conquistador Hernando de Soto landed in the Spanish colony of Florida in 1539 and marched north with six hundred soldiers. De Soto had been among a party that had found a wealth of gold in Peru, South America, a few years earlier. He hoped to do the same in North America. De Soto entered what is now Georgia in 1540. At first the Creek and the descendants of the Mound Builders were friendly to the strangers, but the Spaniards' cruelty soon hardened the Indians. While some Indians were killed in fighting with the Spaniards, many more died from the diseases de Soto and later explorers brought with them from Europe. The Indians had no immunity to these diseases. It is estimated that smallpox alone killed one in three Indians in the Southeast. The Mound Builders never recovered from this disaster. The last of the civilization joined other tribes, such as the Creek and Cherokee.

De Soto and his party met with their own disaster. They crossed the Savannah River and continued north, where they found pearls and copper, but no gold. Frustrated but persistent, de Soto headed farther north, into what is now the Carolinas. Exhausted and sick with fever, he died on the banks of the Mississippi River in 1542. His men secretly buried him on the river

Following his death, Hernando de Soto was secretly buried in the Mississippi River.

bottom at night. They feared the Indians would attack if they knew their leader was dead.

De Soto's expedition was a failure, but the Spaniards did not give up on Georgia. It may have had no gold, but its location, just north of their Florida colony, was important strategically. In 1566 Pedro Menéndez de Avilés established the first Spanish fort and mission in Georgia on Saint Catherines Island. Other outposts quickly followed along the Georgia coast. They were meant to defend Georgia against the French, who had established their own colony in Florida in 1564. Within a century most of the Spanish forts and missions had been abandoned, the inhabitants driven out by the British and their Creek and Cherokee allies.

In the late 1600s and early 1700s Georgia waters became a favorite haunt for such notorious pirates as Edward Teach, better known as Blackbeard. To this day some fortune hunters believe the pirate's treasure lies buried somewhere on Blackbeard Island, his headquarters on the Georgia coast, which is now a national refuge.

Edward Teach, better known as Blackbeard (shown on the right), was one of the most feared and despised pirates of all time.

THE GROWING COLONY

In the early 1700s Georgia remained a kind of no-man's-land between the British colonies to the north and Spanish Florida to the south. Its fate was altered forever by an English aristocrat with a social conscience—James Edward Oglethorpe. Oglethorpe represented a group of men who wanted to help the English poor, especially those condemned to debtors' prison, where people who couldn't pay their debts were confined. In 1730 they asked King George II for land in North America where such unfortunate people could start a new life. King George was impressed for two reasons: the new colony would be named the Province of Georgia in his honor, and it would provide a strategic buffer between the English Carolinas and Spanish Florida. In 1732 Oglethorpe and thirty-five hardworking but needy families sailed for North America.

After reaching South Carolina eighty-eight days later, Oglethorpe traveled up the Savannah River in a small boat. "I fixed upon a healthy situation about ten miles from the sea," he wrote to the king. "The river here forms a half-moon, along the south side of which the banks are about forty foot high, and on the top flat." There, Oglethorpe laid out the town of Savannah. A contemporary city planner has called Savannah "one of the finest diagrams for city organization and growth in existence."

Savannah and the colony that grew up around it were to be, in Oglethorpe's words, "a model of virtue." Slavery was not allowed, as it was in other English colonies, and liquor was forbidden. There was freedom of religion for some groups. Each settler would receive 50 acres (20 ha) of land to farm. This generous offer brought several thousand settlers to the colony over the next two decades. They came not only from England but also from Scotland, Germany, Switzerland, and Italy. A group of Jewish immigrants arrived in 1733 and established the third-oldest Jewish congregation in the Americas.

This growth alarmed the Spaniards in Florida, who went to war against the British colony in 1739. Oglethorpe proved to be as fine a military leader as he was a colony builder. He boldly led his militia in a siege on Saint Augustine, the Spanish stronghold in Florida. Two years later the Spaniards launched a sea attack on Britain's Fort

James Oglethorpe led his troops to successfully battle the Spanish in neighboring Florida.

Frederica on Saint Simons Island. The Spanish forces far outnumbered the British, and feeling confident, they stopped to have lunch in a grassy marsh on the island. But they were surprised by British troops in what has come to be called the Battle of Bloody Marsh. The battle was minor but decisive; the Spaniards were never again a threat to the British in North America, although they held on to Florida until 1819.

By 1740 Georgia was well established as a colony, but it was not to remain the model of virtue that its founder envisioned. While many people in England praised Oglethorpe as the Father of Georgia, many disgruntled settlers called him Our Perpetual Dictator. They wanted to enlarge their farms, and for that they needed the cheap labor that slavery could provide. In 1743 Oglethorpe left Georgia and returned to England. Seven years later the colony's trustees reluctantly allowed slavery.

Georgia's farms produced rice, indigo, hogs, cotton, and tobacco, and the colony grew. By 1776 the colony's population was 40,000, nearly half of whom were African-American slaves.

LOYALISTS AND PATRIOTS

Georgia landowners owed much of their wealth to their trade with England, so when northern colonies talked of revolution in the 1770s, most Georgians opposed the idea. Some would remain Loyalists—active supporters of the king—throughout the Revolutionary War. In March 1776 British warships entered the Savannah River. They seized rice that was loaded on local boats and helped royal governor James Wright, who had been under house arrest, escape. These events forced many Georgians to choose sides and join the fight. Some members of the Creek Indian Nation supported the English, while others supported the Americans.

In December 1778 British and Loyalist forces took Savannah. The British promised freedom to Georgia's slaves, and more than one-third of them, approximately five thousand, escaped across the British lines. Savannah would remain in British hands until troops led by General "Mad Anthony" Wayne drove out the enemy in July 1782. A year later the war ended, and the colonies were free.

The patriot soldiers were greatly outnumbered by the British in the Battle of Savannah.

COTTON IS KING

The war left Georgia devastated. In April 1786 the Creek declared war on Georgia, hoping to win back some of the land they had lost over the years. They were led by Alexander McGillivray, a colorful figure whose father was a Scot and whose mother was half Creek. His efforts to unite the southeastern tribes failed however, and in 1790 McGillivray traveled to New York to sign a treaty ceding, or transferring, nearly all of Georgia to the new United States.

To help settle the sparsely populated state, the new state government gave Georgians who fought on the American side in the Revolution free land. New immigrants were also welcomed, causing a second influx of people from other states and Europe.

Among the newcomers was a young man from Connecticut, Eli Whitney, who arrived in Savannah in 1793. Whitney came to Georgia to work as a schoolteacher, but he was also an inventor. "I heard much said of the extreme difficulty of ginning cotton [clearing cotton bolls of seeds]," he wrote in a letter to his parents, "and struck at a plan, a machine with which one man will clean ten times as much cotton as he can in any other way."

Eli Whitney's cotton gin, which he invented in Georgia, cleaned 50 pounds (23 kilograms) of cotton lint a day.

COTTON-PICKING FOLKLORE

Cotton was an integral part of life on Georgia plantations in the 1800s. In the black community much folklore grew up around cotton and its magical properties. Here are a few of these sayings:

If a newly married couple sleeps on a cotton mattress on their wedding night, they will always have money.

If the same couple finds a twin cotton boll, they will have twins within the year.

If an unmarried girl finds a twin cotton boll, she will soon be asked to marry.

When fishing, place twenty dried cottonseeds at the water's edge to guarantee a good catch.

Not all cotton folklore was pure imagination. African Americans' use of cotton as a treatment for toothaches, headaches, and other ailments was based on scientific fact. Gossypol, a poisonous yellow pigment found in cotton, has medicinal properties and has been used in small doses to effectively fight such diseases as malaria. Large doses can be deadly, however, and some animals have died after eating cotton bolls.

Whitney's cotton gin was a boon for the South. Cotton could be cleaned much faster than it had been by hand, and it quickly became the principal crop of Georgia and other southern states. Cotton plantations grew larger, and so did the number of slaves needed to pick cotton in the fields. By the 1820s Georgia was the world's largest grower of cotton.

But this newfound prosperity was not shared by everyone. For two groups—African-American slaves and American Indians—it meant only more trouble. The Creek and Cherokee had adapted well to the ways of the European settlers, but now they stood in the way of "progress." The government wanted their remaining lands for settlement. In 1825 the Creek were forced to give up their land and move to Arkansas. Then, in June 1838, soldiers forced the Cherokee off their land. One soldier described rounding up the Cherokee:

Two or three [Cherokee] dropped their hoes and ran as fast as they could when they saw the soldiers coming into the fields. . . . Chickens, cats, and dogs all ran away when they saw us. Ponies under the shade trees fighting the flies with the noise of their bells; the cows and calves lowing to each other; the poor dogs howling for their owners; the open doors of the cabins as we left them—to have seen it all would have melted to tenderness a heart of stone.

The Cherokee were forced west to Indian Territory, which later became the state of Oklahoma. The thousand-mile (1,609-km) journey took six torturous months. Nearly a quarter of the 14,000 Cherokee died from exposure and exhaustion along the way. The route became known as the Trail of Tears.

THE CIVIL WAR

By 1860 Georgia had become home to 460,000 slaves—nearly eight times the number in 1800. Although more than half of all farmers had no slaves, the slavery system was the backbone of the cotton industry.

That same year Abraham Lincoln, a northerner and a member of the Republican Party, was elected president. Lincoln opposed slavery, although he did not immediately seek to abolish it. Southerners were afraid of what Lincoln might do to change their way of life. It was not simply the issue of slavery that mattered but the right of states to do what they wanted without the interference of the federal government. Southern states began seceding, or breaking away, from the Union. On January 19, 1861, Georgia became the fifth state to secede. These states formed their own union, the Confederate States of America, and elected Jefferson Davis as their president and Georgian Alexander H. Stephens as their vice president. Ironically, Stephens, a former congressman, had previously spoken out strongly against seceding.

By 1860 slavery had become the backbone of the cotton industry.

GOOBER PEAS

The diet of soldiers in the Confederate army deteriorated in the last days of the Civil War. Goober peas are peanuts, which in many cases became the staple food for the rebels—to the point where Georgia soldiers were known as "goober grabbers."

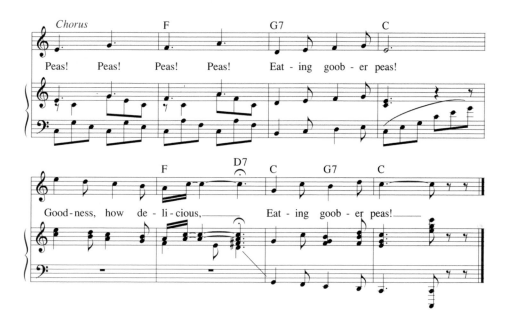

When a horseman passes, the soldiers have a rule,
To cry out their loudest, "Mister, here's your mule!"
But another pleasure, enchantinger than these,
Is wearing out your grinders, eating goober peas! *Chorus*

Just before the battle the General hears a row,
He says, "The Yanks are coming, I hear their rifles now."
He turns around in wonder, and what do you think he sees?
The Georgia Militia—eating goober peas! *Chorus*

I think my song has lasted almost long enough,
The subject's interesting, but rhymes are rough.
I wish this war was over, when free from rags and fleas,
We'd kiss our wives and sweethearts and gobble goober peas. *Chorus*

The Civil War erupted on April 12, 1861, when Confederate forces attacked Fort Sumter in South Carolina's Charleston Harbor. Georgia played an important role in the war, supplying about 120,000 Confederate soldiers. One of the most industrialized of the Southern states, Georgia's factories supplied the Confederate army with much-needed wagons, clothing, and other goods. Atlanta, established in 1837, had grown into a major city by the Civil War. Its many railroad lines made it a transportation hub for the Confederacy.

Georgia saw little action in the first two years of the war, but in September 1863 Confederates won an important victory at the Battle of Chickamauga. As the war continued, however, the South saw fewer and fewer victories. General William Tecumseh Sherman lay siege to Atlanta in the summer of 1864. After six months of fighting, Confederate troops abandoned the city, and Sherman burned much of it to the ground.

General William Tecumseh Sherman's infamous march to the sea, cut a path of destruction across the state.

According to the twenty-eight-year-old Union captain James Royal Ladd, "the whole business portion of the city was in flames, and notwithstanding the night was dark the blaze illuminated the country for miles."

Sherman proceeded to march from Atlanta toward the coast. His "march to the sea" ended six weeks later, in Savannah. Sherman's troops had destroyed everything in their path—farms, towns, and railroad tracks. They had effectively torn the South in two and weakened the will of the Southern people to continue fighting. The war ended the following spring in Union victory.

RECONSTRUCTION

Georgia, like other Confederate states, was occupied by Union troops during the postwar period known as Reconstruction. Northern opportunists, called carpetbaggers because they carried their belongings in cheap carpetbags, took advantage of the situation to control the state government. African Americans, now freed from slavery, were given the right to vote and run for public office. Resentful, white Georgians joined a secret organization called the Ku Klux Klan (KKK), meant to instill fear in African Americans and outsiders. Although slavery had ended, racism had not. Many African Americans, persecuted and unable to make a living by farming, moved to northern cities, where industrial jobs were more plentiful.

Atlanta was rebuilt and replaced Milledgeville as the state capital in 1868. It was the site of the World's Fair and Great International Cotton Exposition in 1881. Atlanta became known as the showcase of the New South, because it could compete economically with the industrialized North.

NEW SOUTH, OLD PROBLEMS

The economy of the New South, like that of the Old South, was built on cotton. African Americans and many poor whites became part of the sharecropping system, whereby they were hired to work the land for landowners who would give them a share of the land's profits. But many landowners took advantage of their workers. Here, an African-American sharecropper named Ed recalls his experiences in the early 1900s:

Mr. Prince [landowner] said he'd loan me ten dollars a month. . . . Then, on shares, the boss furnish you with the land, mule, seeds, tools, and one half of the fertilizer. . . . Things went all right for a while. I was the best cotton picker there. . . . But hard work didn't get me nowhere. Mr. Prince wouldn't show me the papers the gin and the warehouse give him, so I didn't know what the crop had brung and what my share should be. He took his share and all of mine and claim I owe him twenty-four dollars in addition.

But Georgia's landowners and cotton farmers were about to take a fall. In 1895 the price of cotton plummeted. Farmers started growing other crops, such as pecans and peaches, along with cotton, to make a living. By the 1920s they faced another problem. An insect called the boll weevil had invaded the South, eating cotton bolls and destroying much of their crop. Georgia's economy grew worse when the Great Depression struck in the 1930s.

Georgia remained one of the poorest states through the first half of the twentieth century. African-American Georgians stayed at the bottom of the social and economic order, held back by segregation, the separation of black and white people in housing, in jobs, and at such public facilities as restrooms, drinking fountains, and swimming pools. However, some white Georgians boldly stood up against racial injustice. In the 1940s prosecutor Lawrence D. Duke won the conviction of two white Klansmen for flogging a black man, who later died from his injuries. Governor Eugene Talmadge announced he would grant clemency to the two killers. Duke was enraged and went to a public hearing, which the governor was attending, carrying two whips, one of which was used to kill the man. Duke held the whip up to the governor's face and denounced the decision. Shortly after, Talmadge reversed his decision, and the killers went to prison.

Other people in public office were trying to improve life in Georgia. Governor Ellis Arnall, who took office in 1943, cleaned up corruption in state government and abolished the poll tax that had kept African-American Georgians from voting.

Long denied their voting rights, African Americans lined up to vote in the Georgia Democratic primaries in 1946.

MODERN TIMES

Georgia's economy got a big boost during World War II, as local defense plants and other manufacturers hired thousands of workers to meet the demand for wartime products. The 1950s were a time of great change. Northern companies started moving south to take advantage of the warm climate, lower taxes, and large labor force. More and more Georgians were leaving farms and rural areas to find better-paying jobs in towns and cities. By 1960 more people worked in manufacturing jobs than in agriculture.

This same era saw the birth of the civil rights movement, as African Americans and some whites who supported them protested peacefully in marches, sit-ins, and other demonstrations, demanding their full rights as citizens. The movement was led by the Reverend Martin Luther King Jr., who was raised in Atlanta. The violent reaction of the police and racist groups to these nonviolent protests drew national attention to the civil rights movement and led to the enactment of new federal laws against segregation.

Having won their right to vote, black Georgians began voting African Americans into office. In 1965 Julian Bond, a civil rights leader, was elected to the state house of representatives. Other representatives, however, refused to allow Bond to be seated, because he opposed the Vietnam War. The Supreme Court found the action illegal, and Bond served ten years in the house of representatives before being elected to the state senate. In 1972 Andrew Young became the first black U.S. congressman from Georgia since Reconstruction. Maynard H. Jackson Jr. was elected mayor of Atlanta in 1973, becoming the first black mayor of a large southern city. In 2001 Shirley Franklin was elected the first female and fourth black mayor of Atlanta.

A young and eager Maynard H. Jackson Jr. was elected the first black mayor of Atlanta in 1973.

A PRESIDENT FROM PLAINS

When Jimmy Carter was nearing the end of his term as governor of Georgia, his mother asked him what he planned to do next.

"I'm going to run for president," he told her.

"President of what?" she replied.

"Momma, I'm going to run for president of the United States, and I'm going to win."

Few Americans outside of his home state had ever heard of Jimmy Carter when he declared his presidential candidacy in 1974. But Carter persisted in his mission with the same steely determination he showed in everything he did in his life. He won the Democratic nomination, and in November 1976, he defeated President Gerald Ford.

One of the few presidents never to have served in the nation's capital before being elected, Carter came to the White House with limited experience. "I spend about half the time being a student," he confessed during his first year in office. But he soon became a leader, especially in foreign affairs. He strengthened America's bonds with China and helped negotiate a historic peace treaty between Israel and its former enemy, Egypt.

In domestic affairs Carter was less successful. The economy foundered during his administration. In 1980 he lost his reelection bid to Ronald Reagan.

Jimmy Carter returned to his home in Plains, Georgia, where he had been a peanut farmer. Since then he has been one of the busiest and most productive ex-presidents in American history. He has helped negotiate during several foreign crises, has worked as a volunteer and spokesperson for Habitat for Humanity, which helps build homes for disadvantaged people, and has written more than a dozen books. In August 1999 Carter and his wife, Rosalynn, each received the Presidential Medal of Freedom for their good works. "Jimmy and Rosalynn Carter have done more good things for more people in more places than any other couple on the face of the earth," said President Bill Clinton during the ceremony. In 2002 Carter won the Nobel Peace Prize in part for his efforts to advance democracy and human rights.

Boxing legend Muhammad Ali lit the Olympic torch at the opening ceremonies of the Atlanta Games in 1996.

Atlanta played host to the world at the 1996 Summer Olympic Games. The games were held in the Olympic Ring, a 3-mile (5-km) circle measured from the center of the city. Former world heavyweight boxing champion Muhammad Ali lit the Olympic torch for the opening ceremonies. A total of 197 nations participated in the games, including, for the first time, Palestine. It was a record at that time. Fourteen countries won their first medals in events. It was a shining moment for a city and a state that continues to look toward a better and brighter future.

Chapter Three

Peoples and Pastimes

Georgia is a state that has reinvented itself time after time, transforming from a land of plantation splendor to dirt poverty, from a segregated society to an integrated one. Georgia is, like Scarlett O'Hara, the heroine of the novel *Gone with the Wind*, a survivor. The ethnic makeup of the state has changed greatly in the last decade, as more and more immigrants have moved into Georgia looking for greater economic opportunities. Whites make up 65 percent of the state's population; African Americans, 30 percent; Latinos (or Hispanics), who can be of any race, 8 percent; and Asians, 3 percent.

AFRICAN AMERICANS

While black Georgians are a majority in some cities, their numbers are shrinking. In Atlanta, for instance, the African-American population dropped by 30,000 from 1982 to 2002. This reverses a trend that began in the 1970s. At that time many black Georgians began returning to their home state from the North, as job opportunities, the economy, and

No doubt about it, Atlanta is a sports loving city.

race relations in Georgia improved. But as African Americans moved into the cities, many white residents left for the suburbs in what came to be "white flight." Now, many middle-class whites are moving back to Atlanta and other cities, into neighborhoods that have been redeveloped and upgraded. They have done so for several reasons. Since many of them work in the cities, they can avoid long commutes from homes in the suburbs. Meanwhile, many African Americans, unable to afford these newly gentrified neighborhoods, have moved to the suburbs where there is less expensive housing and better job opportunities.

While other ethnic groups, particularly Latinos, are replacing blacks in many of Atlanta's poorer neighborhoods, African Americans still remain the largest population group in many parts of central, coastal, and southwestern Georgia.

Race relations have improved greatly in this once-segregated state. A dramatic example of this occurred in 1997 in the Atlanta suburb of Stone Mountain, when Chuck E. Burris was elected the town's first black mayor. Stone Mountain was the scene of the revival of the Ku Klux Klan (KKK) in 1915, and Burris lives in a house once owned by the former mayor and Imperial Wizard of the National Knights of the KKK, James R. Venable. "There's a new Klan in Stone Mountain," Burris points out, "only it's spelled with a C: c-l-a-n, citizens living as neighbors. And I guess I'm the black dragon." The situation in Stone Mountain, which today is about half black, is a classic example of how many people's attitudes toward race have changed in the last generation.

Georgia has a long and distinguished history of cultural and ethnic diversity.

A DISAPPEARING CULTURE

The Gullah (also called Geechee) African Americans of Georgia and South Carolina's lowcountry, including the coastal islands, have a unique culture. The Gullah are the descendants of slaves who were brought to the region from West Africa in the 1700s to work on rice plantations. Unlike other blacks, the Gullah people living on the islands were able to retain their African roots due to their relative isolation from the mainland. The Gullah language, while English-based, includes many African words. Today there are only a few Gullah communities left. Many young people have left the islands for better economic opportunities. Hog Hammock, a prominent Gullah community on Sapelo Island, now has only fifty residents, most of them elderly. While the community belongs to the Gullah descendants, some heirs who have moved away have sold their land to white developers. Whites are building homes and threatening the future of this once all-black community. "I would rather my community be all black," says island historian Cornelia Bailey. "I would rather have my community what it was in the [19]'50s." In 2006 the U.S. Congress designated the Atlantic coast from North Carolina to Florida, the Gullah-Geechee National Heritage Corridor, to help protect the culture of the people living there.

LATINOS

Latinos are the fastest-growing minority in Georgia. In 2006 there were an estimated 650,000 Latinos in the state, not counting illegal immigrants, who experts say may double that figure. In some northern counties Latinos, mostly from Mexico and Central America, are the largest minority. In the town of Dalton, Latinos make up one-third of the population of 22,000. There are many Latino businesses and a Spanish-language radio station. One of the biggest celebrations in Dalton each year is Mexican Independence Day.

Typical of these hardworking Mexican immigrants is Homero Luna. He came to Georgia in 1993 to work in a poultry plant. Six years later he became the successful publisher of *El Tiempo*, a newspaper for Latinos. "We call Georgia our home," Luna says, speaking for his family and friends.

Many native Georgians have welcomed these new arrivals who have boosted the economy of many communities. However, some residents see Latinos, especially the illegal immigrants, as a threat and a burden to taxpayers. They have renamed their state "Georgiafornia," believing that in time it will become as big a haven for illegal immigrants as the state of California. Georgia lawmakers passed the Georgia Security and Immigration Compliance Act in 2006, the strictest state immigration law in the United States to date. It requires citizenship verification of all employees hired by the state and its contractors. It also denies noncitizen employees over the age of eighteen access to medical care and school scholarships.

ASIAN AMERICANS

While Asian Americans make up approximately 3 percent of the state's population, that number is growing rapidly. Georgia has the third-fastest-growing Asian population, after Nevada and South Carolina. Between 1990 and 2000 the number of Koreans in the state grew by 88 percent. Georgia

Today more Asian Americans are coming to Georgia in search of work.

ranks eighth among the states in Vietnamese residents, and Vietnamese is the fifth most spoken language, following English, Spanish, French, and German.

Among prominent Asian Americans in the state are Indian-American Sanjay Gupta, the chief medical correspondent for CNN (Cable News Network), and Charlice Byrd, a member of the Georgia house of representatives. Byrd, who is half Chinese, is a strong advocate for education, public health, and innovation in life sciences. She was named Legislator of the Year in 2007 by the Biotechnology Industry Organization.

GEORGIA CRACKERS AND YANKEE HONKERS

The Old South lives on in Georgia's rural areas, where a shared past and old traditions still loom large. Other Americans have sometimes looked down their noses at rural white Georgians, calling them "crackers" or "rednecks." The term "cracker," referring to ignorant, poor whites, may have originated from the way wagoners cracked whips over their oxen to make them move. "Redneck" refers to the fact that many rural Georgians work outside in the sun, so their necks are often sunburned. Carter Crittenden, an Atlanta investor who grew up in the small town of Shellman, has a more precise definition. "A redneck is someone who didn't graduate or maybe even go to high school and is a laborer," he explains. "They say a redneck is a mean, evil person. But I never met anyone like that growing up in Shellman. And I haven't met anyone like that today."

While many of Georgia's small towns have changed relatively little, its cities, especially Atlanta, have seen tremendous changes in the last few decades, as tens of thousands of northerners have moved in, bringing new companies and businesses. Native Georgians have reacted to this influx of "Yankees" with good humor and a certain uneasiness. "Although I certainly understand somebody from the land of freeze and squeeze wanting to seek asylum here, I also fear I'm losing my city," wrote Georgia humorist Lewis Grizzard. "Will Southerners start dropping the last part of everybody's first name like the honkers [Northerners] do? . . . Will the automobile horn drown out the lilt of 'Georgia on My Mind'? Will grits become extinct? Will corn bread give way to the bagel?"

For their part, displaced northerners have their own regrets about what they left behind. "We had to get used to everything fried," says Diane Rowe, who moved from Connecticut to greater Atlanta with her husband and daughter. "The traffic is bad and the air is polluted. There's some culture here, but we miss New York City and the theater."

On the other hand, the Rowes love the little community they're in and its climate. "It only snowed this winter once and it melted by noon," she recalls. And as transplants the Rowes have lots of company. "I'd say at least half of the people in our community of fifty-seven homes are not native Georgians."

POPULATION DENSITY

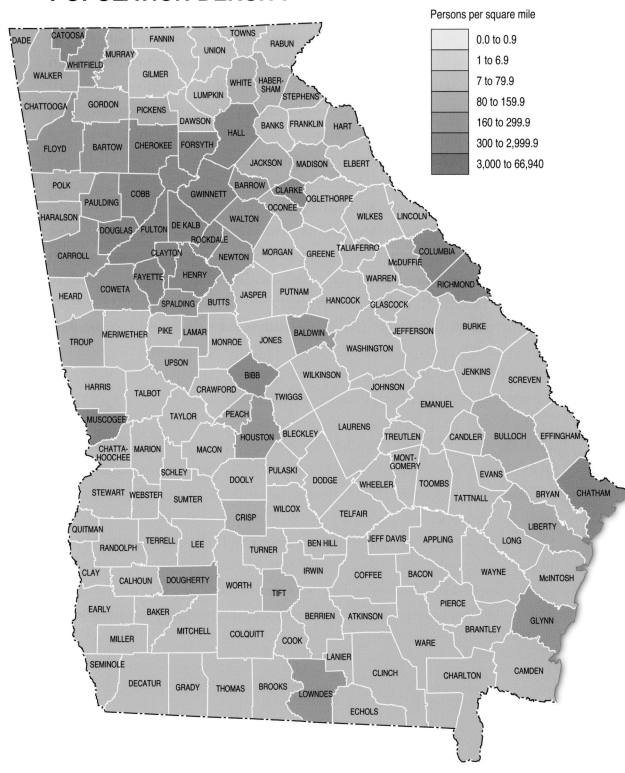

Persons per square mile

	0.0 to 0.9
	1 to 6.9
	7 to 79.9
	80 to 159.9
	160 to 299.9
	300 to 2,999.9
	3,000 to 66,940

BRING ON THE BARBECUE!

If you like barbecued pork, southern style, the place for you is the Big Pig Jig, a barbecue competition and festival held every October in Vienna, about 150 miles (241 km) south of Atlanta. The event draws more than 25,000 barbecue lovers and features a carnival, a parade, a hog-calling contest, and even a 3-mile (5-km) "Hog Jog" run.

But the main event of the festival is the barbecue championship. Teams of barbecuers compete in such categories as Whole Hog, Shoulder, Ribs, Stew, Sauce, and Chicken-Q. In 2007 winning teams sported such colorful names as the Sow Bellies, the Squealer Dealers, the Moonlight Smokers, and the Low Country Longshots.

Whether you come to cook or just fill your belly, you'll agree that the Big Pig Jig is one Georgia tradition made in hog heaven.

EDUCATION

One thing that makes Georgia attractive to newcomers is the public education system. Georgia was a latecomer to public education. Before 1870 "public" schools charged tuition or operated under the generosity of plantation owners. Slave children received little or no schooling. The integration of schools, although mandated by the Supreme Court in 1954, was slow to come to Georgia. Black students first attended previously all-white schools in 1961, and full integration lagged in Georgia for another decade.

In more recent years Georgia has proven to be a leader in education. In 1995 it became the first state to offer free preschool for all four-year-olds. "Pre-K has helped her mature socially," says Greselda McLin-Middleton about her daughter, "and it's really positive because of the multiracial mix of her classmates. . . . It's especially good with so many mothers in the workplace."

But other state education initiatives are not looked on as favorably by parents and the public. In February 2008 rural Greene County announced that in the fall it would become the first school district in the United States to put boys and girls in separate classes. County officials reasoned that single-sex classrooms would help both sexes to focus better on schoolwork, while improving poor test scores and reducing high dropout rates. But many teachers, parents, and students opposed the change and complained that they were not consulted on the matter. "Our movement is about choice," said Leonard Sax, head of the National Association for Single Sex Public Education, who also opposes the move. "One size does not fit all. Even a small school district needs to provide choice." In April 2008 the school board withdrew the plan and hopes to employ the input of parents and teachers to pursue the program in the future. "We decided to go to single gender for one reason and one reason only . . . to help kids get across the finish line," said School Superintendent Shawn McCollough.

Georgia is home to more than one hundred four-year colleges, universities, and other institutes. The largest is the University of Georgia in Athens, which was founded in 1785 as the first state-chartered university in the United States. Emory University, in Atlanta, is perhaps the state's most prestigious private university. There is a long and proud tradition of historically black colleges in Atlanta that includes Morehouse College, which Martin Luther King Jr. attended, and Spelman College.

Georgia believes in providing the best education possible for all of its young citizens.

RELIGION

From the revival meetings of the early Methodist circuit riders to the foot-stomping, gospel-singing black congregations of today, religion has been a joyous and vital part of life in Georgia.

The early colony included a variety of Protestant sects, including the Church of England, Lutheranism, Presbyterianism, and others. The first Baptist church was not founded until 1772, but today Baptist is by far the state's most popular denomination. Methodism is the next most popular

Baptist is Georgia's most popular religious denomination.

church. This is not surprising, since Methodism's founder, John Wesley, accompanied James Oglethorpe to Georgia from England in 1735 and stayed there for two years as a missionary. Today, Georgia also has many Catholic churches and Jewish synagogues.

THE SPORTING LIFE

Georgians are great sports lovers—both as spectators and participants. Atlanta is home to nine professional sports teams. The most famous is baseball's Atlanta Braves. On April 8, 1974, in Atlanta–Fulton County Stadium, Braves' slugger Henry "Hank" Aaron hit his 715th home run, breaking Babe Ruth's record for career homers. The Braves won the World Series for the first time in 1995.

Similar thrills were felt by football fans when the Atlanta Falcons, affectionately known as the Dirty Birds, made it into the Super Bowl for the first time in thirty-three years in 1998. "A chill went through me," recalls Falcons fan Dick West. "Tears got in my eyes. My wife came in and said, 'You all right?' And I was speechless. Then I got over it, and I began to holler. . . . I thought this day would never come." Unfortunately, the Falcons lost to the Denver Broncos.

Every April the Masters Golf Tournament brings the greatest golfers in the world to the National Golf Club in Augusta. The tournament was begun in 1934 by pro-golfing great Bobby Jones.

With forty-five state parks, two national forests, and numerous historic sites, monuments, and seashore areas, Georgia is a great place to get outside. Whether hiking on the Appalachian Trail or racing rubber rafts down the Chattahoochee River, Georgians know how to enjoy the great outdoors. Trout fishing is popular in the northern mountains, and hunting for deer, wild turkey, and duck is popular throughout the state.

Georgia is a great place to get outdoors and enjoy a good game of football played by one of their teams, the Atlanta Falcons.

THE GEORGIA PEACH

Ty Cobb holds the distinction of being one of the greatest baseball players of all time—and one of the most disliked, even by his own teammates. Nicknamed the Georgia Peach early in his career, this was one peach who was anything but sweet.

Cobb was born in Banks County, Georgia, in 1886. His father, who had been both a schoolteacher and a state senator, was a stern taskmaster. When Ty decided on a baseball career against his father's wishes, the elder Cobb told him, "Don't come home a failure." These were words that the young Cobb never forgot. He spent the next twenty-five years working to be the very best in his sport.

Soon after signing with the Detroit Tigers in 1905, Cobb began proving himself a superb hitter, an excellent outfielder, and a whiz at stealing bases. When he retired in 1928, he had a career batting average of .366. His 4,191 career hits remained the major-league record for fifty-seven years, until Pete Rose of the Cincinnati Reds broke it in 1985. All in all, Cobb set forty-three major-league regular-season records, some of which remain unbroken to this day. Cobb was one of the first five players elected to the National Baseball Hall of Fame.

A great athlete, Cobb was less than a great human being. He was aggressive and mean-spirited on and off the field, even to his teammates. Baseball and shrewd investments made Cobb rich, but he was not happy. He did little in his retirement, except play golf and make enemies. Whatever people thought of Ty Cobb, they remained in awe of his baseball skills and his total commitment to the game. As he once told a sports writer, "Baseball was one hundred percent of my life."

THE ARTS—FINE AND FOLK

Culture is one of the jewels in the crown of the Empire State of the South. Atlanta is home to many cultural institutions. The Woodruff Arts Center houses the High Museum of Art, the Alliance Theatre Company, and the Atlanta Symphony Orchestra, along with the 14th Street Playhouse and the Atlanta College of Art. Theaters, museums, and symphony orchestras abound in Georgia's large cities and towns. The state has also been home to some of the greatest rock and rhythm and blues artists of the 1950s and 1960s, including Little Richard, Ray Charles, and Otis Redding.

The High Museum of Art, in Atlanta, Georgia, holds more than 11,000 works in its permanent collection.

SOUL SINGER

Macon, Georgia, has produced a number of gifted popular singers, among them Otis Redding, whom many people consider the greatest soul singer of the 1960s.

Redding was born in Dawson, Georgia, in 1941 and sang in church choirs as a youth. While still in his teens, he made his first recordings but found little success. A few years later he got a job driving a Macon singing group to their gigs. One day he drove them to Memphis for an audition with Stax Records. After the group auditioned, they remembered that Otis sang, too, and they encouraged the shy young man to record one of his songs for Stax president Jim Stewart. Redding sang a slow, soulful ballad he had written called "These Arms of Mine." Stewart was impressed and released the record. It became a hit, the first of many hit records Otis Redding would make at Stax.

Redding's career was taking off when he set off on a tour of the Midwest in December 1967. One cold night his private plane crashed into a frozen lake near the airport at Madison, Wisconsin. Redding and four members of his backup band were killed. Three days earlier he had recorded a thoughtful ballad, "(Sittin' on) The Dock of the Bay," a song he had cowritten. It quickly became the number-one record in America, Otis Redding's only chart-topper. He was twenty-six years old at the time of his death.

In rural Georgia another kind of art is thriving—folk art. Georgia's folk furniture, ceramics, and textiles are experiencing a boom in popularity among art collectors and museums. Georgia folk pottery is particularly popular, with its characteristic humor and eccentricity. A good example is face jugs, which bear expressive and sometimes grotesque human faces.

Georgia folk art is known for its originality.

Folk art is often a family tradition in Georgia. Meansville folk potter Marie Rogers's husband, his father, and his grandfather were all potters. "When they'd leave the house to go to their regular jobs, I'd sit there and try and try," she says. "I was playing with them pottery wheels. Finally I got it and I was real proud of myself." Rogers's pottery includes ring jugs of all kinds, busts, and barnyard animals, such as roosters and pigs.

Not all the artists in rural Georgia, however, are folk artists. The Stillmoreroots Group, formed in 2002, is composed of eight professionally trained artists who display their work in a pine forest. They hold their annual "Art in the Woods" show in the small town of Stillmore in southeastern Georgia. "People who may not be able to go to a big city to see artwork can see art in their own backyard," says Nick Nelson, a member of the group. "Many of our works are installations, like big sculptures that people can walk through. Some of them are even made out of things found in the forest, like pinecones and rocks. Usually artists send their art to a gallery and rarely meet the people who look at their work. Shows like 'Art in the Woods' are really about audience participation and interaction. This makes for a rich experience for both the audience and the artists."

Chapter Four

For the People

Over the years Georgia has had its political ups and downs. In the past the issue of race has divided people more often than it has united them. Corruption has sometimes been a problem in state politics. But Georgia also has a tradition of reform and innovation. In 1922 Rebecca L. Felton of Georgia became the first female U.S. senator. In 1943 Georgia became the first state to grant the right to vote to eighteen-year-olds. After a century of segregation, black voters have become more powerful, electing to office both blacks and whites who have their best interests at heart.

INSIDE GOVERNMENT

Georgia's government, like every state's, is divided into three branches: executive, legislative, and judicial.

Executive

The chief executive of Georgia is the governor, who is elected to a four-year term. The governor makes appointments to state boards and agencies, proposes the state's budget, and approves or vetoes (rejects) laws made by the state legislature. The legislature can override the veto if two-thirds

The Georgia State Capitol, in Atlanta, is an architecturally and historically significant building. It has been named a National Historic Landmark and is listed on the National Register of Historic Places.

of each house agrees. In 2003 Sonny Perdue became the first Republican governor to be elected in the state in 130 years.

Legislative

Georgia's legislative branch is called the general assembly and consists of two houses: a senate with 56 members and a house of representatives with 180 members. Members of both houses are elected to two-year terms. The legislature works on new laws and helps the governor work out the state budget each year.

Judicial

Georgia's highest court is the state supreme court. Its seven justices are elected for six-year terms. The supreme court evaluates whether laws violate the state constitution and whether cases from lower courts were properly

Upon his inauguration in January 2003, Sonny Perdue became the first Republican governor of Georgia since the 1870s.

handled. The next highest court is the court of appeals, which reviews cases in which the losing side questions a lower court's ruling. Its nine judges are also elected for six-year terms. Judges on superior courts, which hear many kinds of criminal and civil cases, are elected to four-year terms.

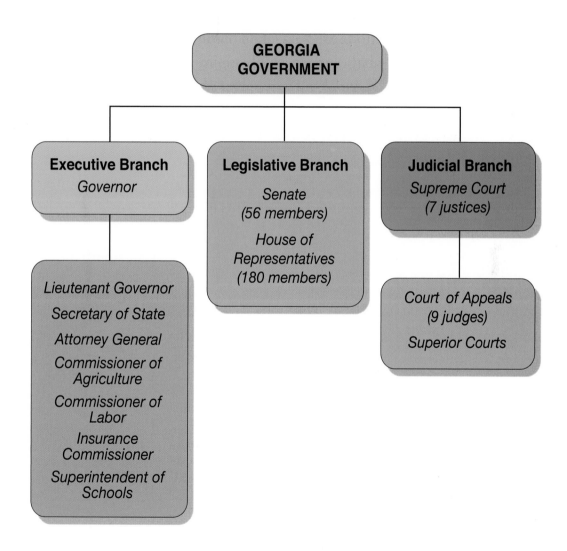

ATLANTA'S FIRST FEMALE MAYOR

Shirley Franklin's motto is to engage in "politics that include, not divide." As mayor of a city that is becoming more diverse every year, her motto has held her in good stead.

Politics and social action have been in Franklin's blood from the start. Born in Philadelphia in 1945, she attended the historically black Howard University and worked there as a civil rights activist in the 1960s. She moved to Atlanta in 1972 and lived in a house on the city's southwest side, where she still lives today. After raising three sons, she served as the city's commissioner of cultural affairs and then as city manager. She was a member of the team that worked to bring the 1996 Summer Olympics to Atlanta.

Elected mayor in 2002, Democrat Franklin has worked hard to build strong ties with the city's whites, Latinos, and Asian Americans. In her first term she managed to overhaul the city's deplorable sewage and water systems without steep increases in rates. She has worked to keep Atlanta affordable for newcomers as well as for African-American families struggling to stay there. Mayor Franklin has earned high praise from many people for returning respectability and responsibility to local government. As proof of her popularity, she was reelected in 2005 with 91 percent of the vote. "To me the question is, will Atlanta be a progressive city, given that it's the home of the civil rights movement, the home of the historic black colleges?" she has said. "Will that continue with the demographic shifts? And my answer is yes."

GEORGIA BY COUNTY

Georgia is one of many southern states that supports gun rights.

GUN CONTROL

The right to bear arms is a popular topic of debate in Georgia. The National Rifle Association (NRA) claims to have 90,000 members in the state. And the tide may be turning against those who support gun control. Atlanta, which has a high crime rate, was one of twenty-eight American cities that sued the gun industry in 1999 for failure to install adequate warnings or safety devices on their firearms. The NRA, together with gun companies, countered by lobbying to make such lawsuits illegal. "Georgia is a strong Second-Amendment state," claims Republican state senator Eric Johnson. "People here see any attempt to sue gun manufacturers as an attempt to restrict the citizens' right to keep and bear arms." However, in October 1999 a Georgia judge ruled that a city could sue gun manufacturers.

In 2008 Georgia lawmakers relaxed existing gun laws in the state, including the law banning the carrying of concealed weapons on public transportation and in restaurants serving alcohol. In light of these changes anti–gun control groups, such as GeorgiaCarry.org, have challenged the ban that still exists on carrying concealed firearms in Atlanta's parks and even in the terminal of the Hartsfield-Jackson Atlanta International Airport. Airport director Benjamin R. DeCosta has refused to change the terminal's ban on firearms. "We want to make sure the airport is safe and secure," he has said. "My belief is if the legislature believed this would allow people to bring guns to the busiest airport in the world, they never would have passed it." A federal judge agreed with the airport, but GeorgiaCarry.org is appealing the decision.

Chapter Five

Working Together

Georgia's economy in 2007 was one of the healthiest in the United States. The total gross state product was a walloping $396 billion. Income per capita in 2005 was $40,155, the tenth highest in the nation. Once based primarily on agriculture, Georgia's economy is focused firmly on service and high-tech industries. Fewer than 3 percent of Georgia's workers are employed in agriculture.

AGRICULTURE AND NATURAL RESOURCES

Farming is still important in the state. Georgia is number one among the states in the production of peanuts, pecans, lima beans, and pimiento peppers. So many peaches are grown in Georgia that it is nicknamed the Peach State, and many streets in Atlanta and elsewhere contain the word "peach." Other important crops include wheat, soybeans, tobacco, and, of course, cotton. The state also ranks first in the production of young chickens raised for eating, known as broilers. Other chickens are raised for laying eggs, another important agricultural product in Georgia.

Georgia grows nearly half of all of the peanuts produced in the United States.

THE ONION STATE?

When people think of Geor-
gia, they usually imagine
tasty peanuts, juicy peaches,
or plump pecans. But sweet
onions? Unlikely! Before you
turn up your nose at Georgia
onions, however, consider
those grown in Vidalia, in the
southeastern part of the state.

Vidalia onions have been called the caviar of onions.
Unlike others, they are sweet, not bitter. They are so sweet that
people eat them raw on sandwiches or chop them up to put
into marmalade.

Onions weren't always so highly prized in Georgia. Georgia
farmers had first noticed the onions' unique flavor in the 1930s,
but it wasn't until 1974 that they really became popular. That year
Delbert Bland talked his father into replacing their failed tomato
crop with onions. Through clever marketing and hard work, Bland
made Vidalia onions famous and turned the family onion farm
into an international business with more than 125 employees.
Today more than 150 onion growers work in the region.

And what makes Vidalia onions so sweet? Experts say
the sweet taste comes from the low sulfur content of southeastern Georgia's sandy soil.

By comparison, fishing is a modest industry in Georgia and consists of such shellfish as crabs, shrimps, and oysters. Brunswick, in the southeastern corner of the state, is one of the South's most important seafood processing centers.

Georgia's pine forests are the mainstay of a thriving lumber industry. The state is the biggest producer of lumber and pulpwood east of the Mississippi. It also ranks first in the nation in the production of turpentine, a liquid from pine trees used in making disinfectants, insecticides, and other chemical products.

Georgia is a leading producer of lumber and pulpwood.

PEANUT BUTTER CORN MUFFINS

Georgians use peanuts in just about everything. And why not? They have so many of them! Have an adult help you make this delicious treat, which will liven up any meal.

$^3/_4$ cup flour
1 $^1/_2$ cups cornmeal
4 teaspoons baking powder
1 teaspoon salt
2 eggs, beaten
1 $^1/_4$ cups milk
$^1/_4$ cup salad oil
jar of crunchy peanut butter

Put the flour, cornmeal, baking powder, and salt into a mixing bowl, and blend with an electric mixer. Add eggs, milk, and salad oil to the mixture, and blend until smooth.

Put 2 tablespoons of the mixture into the bottom of each cup of a greased muffin pan. Add 1 tablespoon of crunchy peanut butter to each cup. Add the remaining mixture to fill each cup.

Bake at 400 degrees Fahrenheit (204 degrees Celsius) for thirty minutes. Allow to cool, and then dig in!

Mining is less important, despite the state's wealth of minerals. Georgia produces more granite than any other state, and the town of Elberton is known as the Granite Capital of the World. Georgia dimension granite has been a popular building material since it was used in the construction of the U.S. Capitol in Washington, D.C. Marble is another popular material used in making buildings, monuments, and gravestones that are found in the state. But perhaps Georgia's most valuable mineral is a rare kind of white clay called kaolin, which is dug out of large pits located near the cities of Augusta and Macon. Kaolin is a key ingredient in paint, plastics, rubber, and the coated paper used in magazines.

A technician works at a kaolin mixer. Kaolin is a naturally deposited clay used in the manufacturing of ceramics, as well as in coatings for paper and textiles.

INDUSTRY AND TECHNOLOGY

Textiles are Georgia's leading manufactured product. Textile mills in Augusta, Columbus, Rome, and Macon produce such varied materials as corduroy, terry cloth, and velvet. Dalton, in northern Georgia, produces more than half of the world's tufted carpets.

2007 GROSS STATE PRODUCT: $396 Million

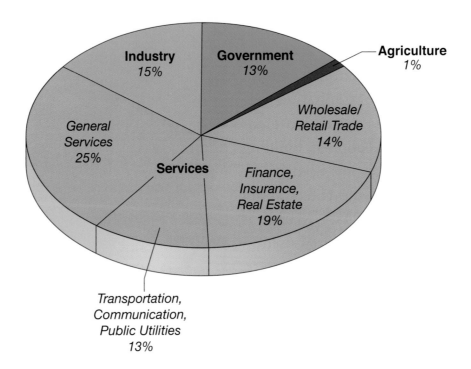

Some of the biggest businesses in the nation have their corporate headquarters in Georgia. They include United Parcel Service (UPS), Home Depot, Delta Airlines, and Coca-Cola, which is based in Atlanta. Coke is the most popular soft drink in the world. The beverage was first concocted in a brass kettle by Atlanta pharmacist John S. Pemberton in 1886. It was sold as a medicine to relieve such common ailments as headaches, indigestion, and sluggishness. The secret formula for Coke has remained closely guarded over the years. Charles Howard Candler, son of Asa Candler, who bought the business after Pemberton's death in

1891, recalled the time his father shared the secret formula with him. "No written formulae were shown. Containers of ingredients, from which the labels had been removed, were identified only by sight, smell, and remembering where each was put on the shelf. To be safe, Father stood by me several times while I compounded these distinctive flavors."

Today the formula for Coca-Cola resides in a safe-deposit vault in the SunTrust Banks in Atlanta, the bank that controls the company stock.

The Coca-Cola Company, headquartered in Atlanta, is the world's largest beverage company.

MEDIA MOGUL

In a world of cautious corporate executives, Ted Turner is a colorful adventurer, whose gambles have made him rich and successful.

Robert Edward Turner III was born in Cincinnati, Ohio, in 1938. His father owned a billboard advertising company. When Ted was eight years old, the family moved to Savannah. Ted was a rebel whose high spirits survived a stretch at a military academy and prep school. He studied economics at Brown University in Rhode Island, where he excelled in debating, sailing, and partying. He was expelled twice.

In 1960 Turner joined his father's company. Three years later the twenty-four-year-old Ted took over the business. He not only made it a bigger success than ever but also set out to diversify the company. Against the advice of everyone around him, he bought two failing television stations. He used a clever billboard advertising campaign and innovative programming to turn the stations around. Then he bought two sports teams, the last-place Atlanta Braves baseball team and the Atlanta Hawks basketball team, partly so he could televise their games on his stations. The teams gradually became winners.

In 1976 he risked his growing empire on the new technology of cable television. One of his station's signals was beamed through a space satellite and became Superstation TBS (Turner Broadcasting System). By 1978 it was seen in two million households. Soon after, he launched the Cable News Network (CNN), the first twenty-four-hour all-news network, and bought MGM's library of more than three thousand old movies for more than $1 billion. Both gambles paid off. CNN changed the face of television news, and the movies filled the programming on two new Turner cable networks, Turner Network Television (TNT) and Turner Classic Movies (TCM).

Today, Turner is one of America's wealthiest men and one of its most generous. In 1997 he pledged $1 billion to the United Nations, one of the biggest individual donations ever made.

Known as the Mouth of the South, Ted Turner is notorious for his outspokenness on politics and social issues. But unlike some people, he has backed his words with actions.

In the 1990s Georgia became one of the leading states for high-tech jobs. By 2004 it led the nation in the creation of these jobs, including manufacturing everything from computer parts to automobile transmissions, as well as developing broadband communications, biotechnology, and computer software. According to the American Electronics Association, Georgia was ranked tenth among the states in 2004 for employment in high technology.

"Georgia's technology industry is founded on a rich supply of world-class talent and strong public-private partnerships," according to Governor Sonny Perdue. "The result has been groundbreaking research and development that has yielded technologies that have changed the way people live, work, and play."

Sleek interstate highways and modern train lines link Georgia's towns and cities. Atlanta remains, as it was in Civil War days, the transportation hub of the state and the entire Southeast. It boasts the busiest airport in the nation—Hartsfield-Jackson Atlanta International Airport—one of the busiest ports in the United States.

Hartsfield-Jackson Atlanta International Airport, located south of Atlanta, was the world's busiest airport in 2007.

EARNING A LIVING

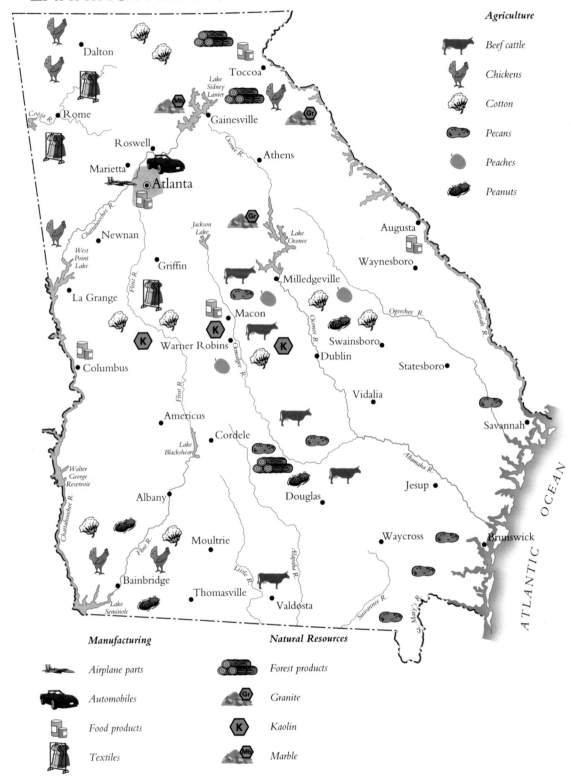

Agriculture

Beef cattle

Chickens

Cotton

Pecans

Peaches

Peanuts

Manufacturing

Airplane parts

Automobiles

Food products

Textiles

Natural Resources

Forest products

Gr Granite

K Kaolin

Mb Marble

Dalton

Toccoa

Lake Sidney Lanier

Rome

Coosa R.

Gainesville

Mb

Gr

Roswell

Marietta

Oconee R.

Athens

Atlanta

Newnan

Chattahoochee R.

West Point Lake

Jackson Lake

Gr

Lake Oconee

Augusta

Waynesboro

Griffin

Milledgeville

La Grange

Flint R.

Macon

K

Warner Robins

K

Ocmulgee R.

Oconee R.

Ogeechee R.

Swainsboro

Savannah R.

Columbus

K

Dublin

Statesboro

Americus

Flint R.

Cordele

Vidalia

Lake Blackshear

Savannah

Walter George Reservoir

Chattahoochee R.

Albany

Douglas

Jesup

Altamaha R.

Moultrie

Flint R.

Waycross

Brunswick

Bainbridge

Little R.

Thomasville

Alapaha R.

Valdosta

Suwannee R.

Mary's R.

Lake Seminole

ATLANTIC OCEAN

WORKING FOR THE GOVERNMENT

Perhaps the largest single employer in Georgia is the federal government. Atlanta is a regional center for federal agencies. The Centers for Disease Control and Prevention (CDC) is also located there. It is the leading federal agency involved in protecting the health and safety of U.S. citizens. It investigates health problems, performs research, and develops public health policies. The CDC also develops and applies disease prevention and control strategies.

GEORGIA WORKFORCE

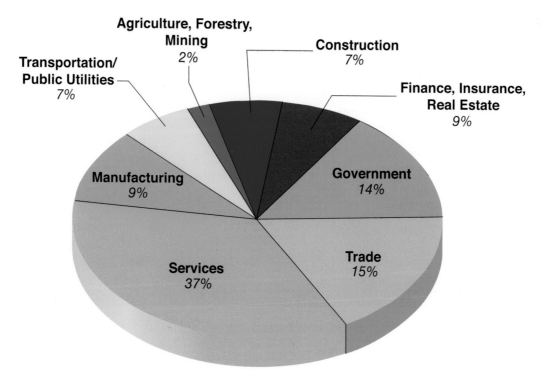

Agriculture, Forestry, Mining
2%

Construction
7%

Transportation/
Public Utilities
7%

Finance, Insurance,
Real Estate
9%

Manufacturing
9%

Government
14%

Services
37%

Trade
15%

There are numerous military installations in the state. The largest is Fort Benning, near Columbus, which was established in 1918 and is home to about 100,000 soldiers. Other major bases are the Naval Submarine Base Kings Bay in southeastern Georgia, which is the Atlantic homeport for U.S. ballistic missile submarines; and the Robins Air Force Base in Houston County, which is the home of Warner Robins Air Logistics Center, a manager for a broad range of aircraft, engines, missiles, software, and electronic and accessory components worldwide.

CYPHER, a robotic helicopter developed for military use, displays its surveillence capabilities at Fort Benning, Georgia.

FIGHTING DISEASE ON THE FRONT LINE

If and when a cure for the deadly disease AIDS (acquired immune deficiency syndrome) is found, the CDC will probably have played a large role in finding it. Headquartered in Georgia's capital since 1946, the organization was formed  to fight malaria and typhus, diseases that at the time threatened residents of the Deep South. Since then the CDC's laboratories have researched and found ways to control and prevent polio, smallpox, Legionnaires' disease, and a host of other infectious diseases. Besides the challenging task of fighting disease, the CDC distributes public health information across the country and serves as a training center for health workers.

The CDC's weekly paper reported the first cases of AIDS in 1981. Six years later it announced the connection between the sometimes fatal disease Reye's syndrome and aspirin use in children. More recently it has taken aim at such chronic diseases as cancer and heart disease. With their successful track record, it is hoped that the dedicated medical workers at the CDC will be able to find better treatments for AIDS and other deadly diseases.

Chapter Six

Georgia Top to Bottom

Georgia is a big state, chock-full of natural beauty, historic sites, rustic small towns, and bustling cities. Let's take a tour of the state from top to bottom.

NORTHERN GEORGIA

Traveling south from Tennessee to the Peach State, our first stop is the site of two major Civil War battles—the Chickamauga and Chattanooga National Military Park. Covering 9,000 acres (3,642 ha) of woods and battlefields in northwestern Georgia and Tennessee, the park was dedicated in 1896 and is the oldest and most intact military park operated by the National Park Service. In September 1863 Union and Confederate troops met at Chickamauga Creek, near the state line, in a fierce battle that resulted in 28,000 casualties. Most of the historical markers and monuments were planned and put in place by veterans of the battle. The Chickamauga Visitors Center features a museum containing three hundred years' worth of American military shoulder arms.

Chickamauga and Chattanooga National Military Park, located in northern Georgia, preserves and commemorates Civil War battlefields.

In Point Park visitors get a grand view of the countryside extending into Tennessee, Alabama, and Georgia. Point Park also houses an observatory and a restored Civil War–era home.

To the east, we find Chattahoochee-Oconee National Forest, the two national forests in the state that are now joined together. Chattahoochee-Oconee's 750,502 acres (303,717 ha) contain at least 135 species of trees, more than any other forest in North America. A few miles south lies Amicalola Falls, the highest waterfall in the state. This cold, crystal-clear mountain creek drops 729 feet (222 m) in seven breathtaking cascades.

Farther south we come to the town of Rome, which like its namesake in Italy, is built on seven hills. In 1929 Italian dictator Benito Mussolini sent a bronze replica of a Roman statue to Rome's sister city in America. The sculpture, depicting the she-wolf that nursed the city's legendary founders, Romulus and Remus, still stands in front of Rome's city hall.

Moving south, we enter the great city of Atlanta. Atlanta has so many treasures that it's hard to know where to begin. One of the most moving places for visitors is the Martin Luther King Jr. National Historic Site. It includes the modest house on Auburn Avenue where King was born, and Ebenezer Baptist Church, where both he and his father preached. At the King Center you can see the slain civil rights leader's white marble tomb, inscribed with words from his famous March on Washington speech: "Free at Last. Free at Last. Thank God Almighty I'm Free at Last." King's Nobel Peace Prize and other personal effects are on display in Freedom Hall.

This marble tomb is just one of the many memorials to visit at the Martin Luther King Jr. National Historic Site.

PLACES TO SEE

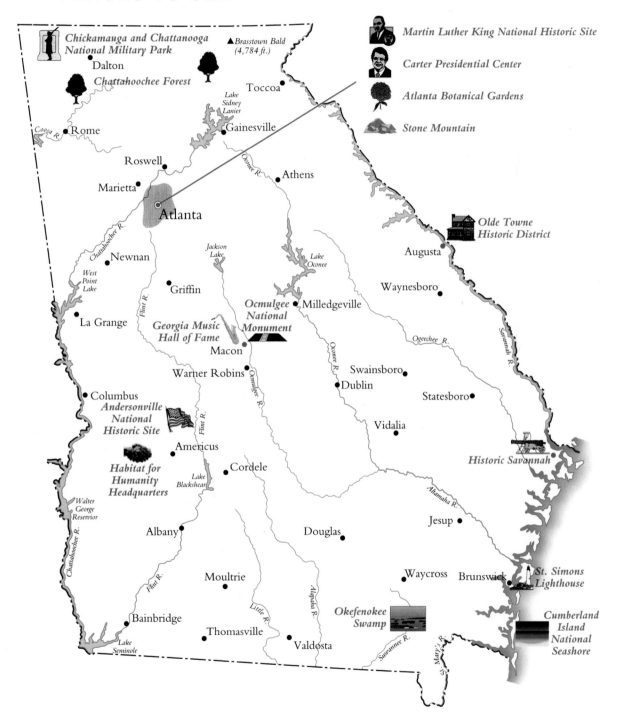

Chickamauga and Chattanooga National Military Park

▲Brasstown Bald (4,784 ft.)

Martin Luther King National Historic Site

Carter Presidential Center

Atlanta Botanical Gardens

Stone Mountain

Dalton

Chattahoochee Forest

Toccoa

Lake Sidney Lanier

Coosa R.

Rome

Gainesville

Oconee R.

Roswell

Athens

Marietta

Atlanta

Chattahoochee R.

Newnan

Jackson Lake

Lake Oconee

Olde Towne Historic District

Augusta

West Point Lake

Griffin

Waynesboro

Flint R.

La Grange

Georgia Music Hall of Fame

Ocmulgee National Monument

Milledgeville

Ogeechee R.

Savannah R.

Macon

Warner Robins

Ocmulgee R.

Oconee R.

Swainsboro

Dublin

Statesboro

Columbus

Andersonville National Historic Site

Flint R.

Vidalia

Americus

Habitat for Humanity Headquarters

Cordele

Lake Blackshear

Altamaha R.

Historic Savannah

Walter George Reservior

Albany

Douglas

Jesup

Chattahoochee R.

Flint R.

Moultrie

Waycross

Brunswick

St. Simons Lighthouse

Bainbridge

Little R.

Alapaha R.

Okefenokee Swamp

Cumberland Island National Seashore

Lake Seminole

Thomasville

Valdosta

Suwanee R.

St. Mary's R.

Equally impressive is the Carter Presidential Center, which includes the Museum of the Jimmy Carter Library, built to honor the only Georgian to become president. The Carter Center runs various international programs on human rights and conflict resolution.

When you're tired of museums and historic sites, you might spend an afternoon shopping and eating in the Buckhead section of Atlanta, which writer Florence Fabricant called "the jewel of the city, an area of gracious homes, elegant hotels and shopping centers, as well as some of the best restaurants."

If it's greenery you're looking for, you can hardly do better than the Atlanta Botanical Gardens in Piedmont Park. Its Fuqua Conservatory features many tropical and endangered plants, none rarer than the *Amorphophallus titanium* of Sumatra. The world's largest flowering plant, it has flowered fewer than a dozen times in cultivation in this country. Besides its size, the flower has another claim to fame—its horrible aroma. Tropical plants curator Ron Gagliardo describes the smell of its blossom as "a cross between a dead animal and a rotting pumpkin. You get used to it, but in the first few minutes [of blooming], it was a little nauseating even for me."

A more common but very intriguing plant grows in the city of Athens, to the east. The white oak tree that stands in a town square is respectfully known as the Tree That Owns Itself. Many years ago the tree's owner deeded the tree ownership of itself and all the land within 8 feet (2 m) of its trunk. The original tree fell in a 1942 storm, but another has grown from one of its acorns on the same site. Athens is also home to Georgia's oldest institute of higher learning and the nation's first state-chartered university, the University of Georgia, founded in 1785. It features the Georgia Museum of Art and the Collegiate Tennis Hall of Fame, which honors great college tennis players.

The Atlanta Botanical Gardens houses the world's largest flower, the Amorphophallus titanium, *also known as the corpse flower.*

STONE MOUNTAIN

Just east of Atlanta stands one of the most spectacular creations of nature and humankind—the Stone Mountain monument. Chiseled on this 300-million-year-old granite mountain are the Confederacy's three greatest heroes, mounted on horseback: General Robert E. Lee, General Thomas "Stonewall" Jackson, and President Jefferson Davis. Spreading over almost 3 acres (1 ha) on the north face of the mountain, it is the world's largest sculpture.

The grand work was begun in 1923 but abandoned some years later. Work finally resumed and the sculpture was completed in 1970—fifty-four years after it was first conceived.

A hiking trail winds up to the mountain's summit, but less ambitious visitors can ride a cable car to the top or travel around the mountain on a locomotive from the Civil War era. The mountain is surrounded by a 3,200-acre (1,295 ha) recreational and historical park.

Farther east we enter beautiful Augusta, Georgia's second-oldest city, founded by James Oglethorpe in 1736. The gracious nineteenth- and early-twentieth-century homes of the city's leading citizens have been lovingly restored in the Olde Town Historic District. Augusta was the state capital from 1785 to 1795, but it is better known today for the internationally renowned Masters Golf Tournament, held each April. Other international competitions that bring sports fans and athletes to Augusta include the Augusta Invitational Rowing Regatta and the Augusta Southern Nationals Drag Boat Races.

TEN LARGEST CITIES

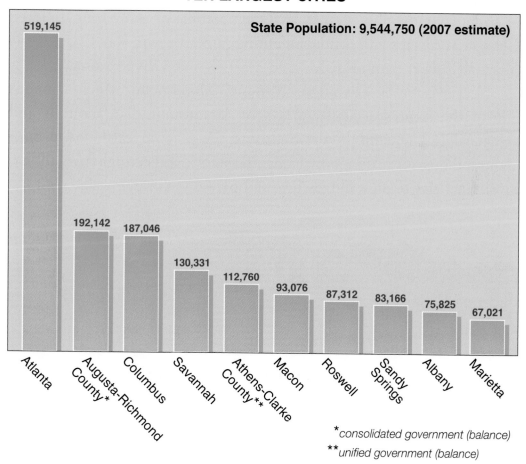

State Population: 9,544,750 (2007 estimate)

- Atlanta — 519,145
- Augusta-Richmond County* — 192,142
- Columbus — 187,046
- Savannah — 130,331
- Athens-Clarke County** — 112,760
- Macon — 93,076
- Roswell — 87,312
- Sandy Springs — 83,166
- Albany — 75,825
- Marietta — 67,021

*consolidated government (balance)
**unified government (balance)

CENTRAL GEORGIA

Macon, Georgia's sixth-largest city, is often called the heart of Georgia because it lies near the state's geographic center. It holds the distinction of being the only southeastern city that can trace its beginnings to a frontier fort, Fort Hawkins, built in 1806. The fort's remains still stand.

Home of poet Sidney Lanier and Wesleyan College, founded in 1831 and the first college chartered to grant degrees to women, Macon is now better known as the rock music capital of Georgia. The Georgia Music Hall of Fame contains photographs and memorabilia of some four hundred Georgia musicians and bands, including James Brown, Ray Charles, the Marshall Tucker Band, R.E.M., and Macon's own Otis Redding.

Near Macon is Ocmulgee National Monument, which contains one of the most spectacular arrays of American Indian mounds and archaeological remains in the Southeast. A restored earth lodge built about a thousand years ago by Indian farmers as a meetinghouse still has its original clay floor, wall benches, and partially standing walls.

American-Indian mounds are preserved at the Ocmulgee National Monument, which is near Macon, Georgia.

Southwest of Macon, along the Chattahoochee River, lies Columbus, Georgia's third-largest city. The river has long been central to the city's life, and Columbus was a thriving river port until the coming of the railroad in the 1830s. Today, seven hydroelectric plants line the river, providing the power for Columbus's many factories. The Columbus Iron Works, which closed in 1964, produced the Confederate ironclad ship the CSS *Jackson/Muscogee*, whose remains are on display at the Woodruff Museum of Civil War Naval History.

SOUTHERN GEORGIA

East of Columbus lies one of the grimmest reminders of the Civil War. It is not a battlefield but a Confederate prison—Andersonville. The most notorious of all Civil War prisons, it once held more than 33,000 Union prisoners of war, although it was built to accommodate only ten thousand. Thousands of prisoners died of diseases spread by the filthy conditions and contaminated water. The Andersonville National Historic Site includes the prison grounds, a national cemetery where more than 16,000 veterans and family members are buried, and the National Prisoner of War Museum, which examines prisoners' experiences in every war our country has fought in.

Just 10 miles (16 km) to the southwest is a reminder of the better side of human nature—the headquarters of Habitat for Humanity International, located in the town of Americus. Founded in 1976, Habitat for Humanity organizes volunteers to build and renovate homes for needy people in the United States and abroad. To date, the organization has provided 65,000 homes for more than 300,000 people. The headquarters contains a museum and tour center and the Habitat

The National Prisoner of War Museum at Andersonville records the experiences of American prisoners of war, from the Revolutionary War to Operation Iraqi Freedom.

for Humanity International Global Village, featuring replicas of fifteen Habitat homes from countries around the world.

Heading eastward to the Atlantic coast brings us to Savannah. The state's oldest city, founded in 1733, Savannah served as the colonial and state capital until 1785. Savannah's rich heritage is alive in its historic downtown, where twenty-two of the twenty-four squares laid out by James Oglethorpe survive. Dotted with gently flowing fountains, majestic live oaks, and historic statues, the squares are a reminder of a quaint and simpler time.

Among the most famous of Savannah's many historic buildings are the Herb House, the oldest standing building in Georgia, built in 1734, and the Pirates' House, a seamen's inn built in the mid-1700s and used by author Robert Louis Stevenson as one of the settings of his classic adventure story *Treasure Island*. Near the Savannah River, bronze tablets memorialize the launching of the SS *Savannah*, which in 1819 became the first steamship to cross the Atlantic Ocean, traveling from Savannah to Liverpool, England. Nearby, visitors can take a cruise on the *Savannah River Queen*, a replica of a stern-wheeler ship from the 1800s.

The Savannah River Queen, *a six hundred passenger red, white, and blue vessel, offers a variety of tours all throughout the harbor.*

THE LITTLE WHITE HOUSE

In 1924 New York politician Franklin Delano Roosevelt, who had been stricken with the crippling disease polio three years earlier, paid a visit to Warm Springs, Georgia, a health resort known for its restorative mineral waters. For several months he swam daily in the soothing waters of Warm Springs. The treatments he received helped restore Roosevelt's sense of well-being and confidence. He returned to politics and in 1928 was elected governor of New York. But he didn't forget Warm Springs. He bought the springs and the land around it and set up the Georgia Warm Springs Foundation. It provided free treatments for polio patients who couldn't afford them.

After Roosevelt was elected president in 1932, he spent so much time at his small white cottage at Warm Springs that it was nicknamed the Little White House. He was there on April 12, 1945, posing for his portrait, when without warning, he collapsed and died.

Roosevelt's cottage at Warm Springs is now a state historic site. Today visitors walk from a memorial fountain to the Franklin Delano Roosevelt Memorial Museum, which is dedicated to Roosevelt's life and achievements. It is both a fine monument to a great American and a special place where he found healing and comfort.

From Savannah it's a short journey to Georgia's famous Golden Isles located along the Atlantic coast. While Saint Simons, Sea, Little Saint Simons, Jekyll, and Tybee islands are favorite destinations for vacationers, lesser-known Sapelo Island, the northernmost isle, has its own charms. Among its sights are the University of Georgia's Marine Institute, the impressive mansion built for tobacco magnate R. J. Reynolds in 1925, and the Gullah-Geechee community of Hog Hammock.

Traveling southwest from the coast we come to Folkston, which lies at the east entrance to the 600-square-mile (1,554-sq-km) Okefenokee Swamp, most of which is a wildlife refuge. Farther west, near the Florida border, is the small town of Thomasville, which was a popular winter resort for wealthy northerners in the late 1800s. One of the most prominent of its winter cottages for the rich is the Lapham-Patterson House on North Dawson Street. Every room in this spacious 1884 mansion is a different shape. It was also one of the first homes in the area to have indoor plumbing and a gas lighting system.

This ends our top-to-bottom tour of Georgia—Peach State, Goober State, and Empire State of the South. For millions of Georgians its best name is simply "home."

THE FLAG: The state flag has three horizontal bars of red and white, with a blue square at the top left. The state seal is centered on the blue square, surrounded by thirteen stars, with the words In God We Trust *underneath.*

THE SEAL: Adopted in 1798, the state seal shows a man holding a sword, standing amid three pillars. This scene represents Georgians' readiness to defend the Constitution. On banners around the pillars are the words Wisdom, Justice, *and* Moderation *from the state motto.*

State Survey

Statehood: January 2, 1788

Origin of Name: Named after King George II of England

Nickname: Empire State of the South; Peach State

Capital: Atlanta

Motto: Wisdom, Justice, and Moderation

Bird: Brown thrasher

Flower: Cherokee rose

Tree: Live oak

Fish: Largemouth bass

Fossil: Shark tooth

Gem: Quartz

Insect: European honeybee

Brown thrasher

Cherokee rose

GEORGIA ON MY MIND

This beautiful song was written in 1930, but it wasn't until Ray Charles performed it before the state legislature on March 7, 1979, that it was adopted as the official state song.

Words by Stuart Gorrell

Music by Hoagy Carmichael

GEOGRAPHY

Highest Point: 4,784 feet (1,458 m) above sea level, at Brasstown Bald

Lowest Point: sea level along the coast

Area: 59,425 square miles (153,910 sq km)

Greatest Distance, North to South: 318 miles (512 km)

Greatest Distance, East to West: about 278 miles (447 km)

Hottest Recorded Temperature: 112 ºF (44 ºC) at Greenville on May 27, 1978

Coldest Recorded Temperature: –17 ºF (–27 ºC) in Floyd County on January 27, 1940

Average Annual Precipitation: 50 inches (127 cm)

Major Rivers: Alapaha, Altamaha, Chattahoochee, Chattooga, Flint, Ocmulgee, Oconee, Ogeechee, Satilla, Savannah, Withlacoochee

Major Lakes: Allatoona, Blackshear, Carters, Clarke's Hill (also known as Thurmond), Hartwell, Oconee, Russell, Seminole, Sidney Lanier, Sinclair, Walter George, West Point

Trees: beech, birch, cedar, cypress, hickory, live oak, magnolia, maple, palmetto, pecan, pine, sweet gum, tupelo, yellow poplar

Wild Plants: crimson trumpet vine, daisy, honeysuckle, laurel, Queen Anne's lace, red sumac, rhododendron, salt grass, violet

Animals: alligator, beaver, black bear, copperhead snake, deer, fox, muskrat, rabbit, raccoon, squirrel, water moccasin, wild boar

Birds: anhinga, blue jay, cardinal, catbird, dove, duck, egret, heron, marsh hen, meadowlark, mockingbird, quail, towhee, vulture, wood thrush

Fish: bass, bream, catfish, drum, eel, mullet, oyster, rainbow trout, shad, shrimp

Endangered Animals: amber darter, Conasauga logperch, Coosa moccasinshell, Etowah darter, fat three-ridge mussel, gray bat, Gulf moccasinshell, hawksbill sea turtle, humpback whale, Indiana bat, Kemp's ridley sea turtle, Kirtland's warbler, leatherback sea turtle, Ochlockonee moccasinshell, oval pigtoe, ovate clubshell, red-cockaded woodpecker, right whale, shinyrayed pocketbook, shortnose sturgeon, southern acornshell, southern clubshell, southern pigtoe, triangular kidneyshell, upland combshell, West Indian manatee, wood stork

Hawksbill sea turtle

Endangered Plants: American chaffseed, black-spored quillwort, Canby's dropwort, Florida torreya, fringed campion, green pitcher-plant, hairy rattleweed, harperella, mat-forming quillwort, Michaux's sumac, persistent trillium, pondberry, relict trillium, smooth coneflower, Tennessee yellow-eyed grass

Hairy rattleweed

TIMELINE

Georgia History

1400s Creek and Cherokee Indians live in what is now Georgia.

1540 Spaniard Hernando de Soto passes through what is now Georgia.

1733 James Oglethorpe establishes Georgia's first permanent European settlement, in Savannah.

1763 The *Georgia Gazette*, the state's first newspaper, begins publication in Savannah.

1775 The Revolutionary War begins.

1788 Georgia becomes the fourth state.

1793 Eli Whitney develops the cotton gin near Savannah.

1828 Gold is discovered near Dahlonega, setting off America's first gold rush.

1837 Atlanta is founded.

1838 The Cherokee Indians are forced out of Georgia.

1861 Georgia secedes from the Union; the Civil War begins.

1864 Union general William Tecumseh Sherman burns Atlanta.

1868 Atlanta becomes the state capital.

1870 Georgia is readmitted to the Union; the state establishes a system of public schools.

1917–1918 About 95,000 Georgians serve in World War I.

1922 Georgian Rebecca L. Felton becomes the first female U.S. senator; WSB, the first radio station in the South, begins broadcasting in Atlanta.

1941–1945 The United States participates in World War II.

1943 Georgia becomes the first state to extend the vote to eighteen-year-olds.

1948 WSB-TV, the South's first television station, goes on the air in Atlanta.

1964 Georgian Martin Luther King Jr. receives the Nobel Peace Prize.

1973 Atlanta citizens elect Maynard H. Jackson Jr. the first black mayor of a large southern city.

1976 Georgian Jimmy Carter is elected president.

1980 Atlanta resident Ted Turner founds Cable News Network (CNN), the first twenty-four-hour all-news television station.

1982 Georgia adopts its tenth and present constitution.

1996 Atlanta hosts the Summer Olympic Games.

2001 African American Shirley Franklin is elected the first female mayor of Atlanta.

2002 Former president Jimmy Carter wins the Nobel Peace Prize.

2003 George Ervin "Sonny" Perdue is inaugurated as the first Republican governor in more than 130 years.

2007 Georgia experiences the start of the worst drought in a century.

2008 A tornado strikes downtown Atlanta in March, causing considerable damage.

ECONOMY

Agricultural Products: apples, beef cattle, chickens, corn, cotton, eggs, hogs, milk, peaches, peanuts, pecans, soybeans, tobacco, watermelons

Manufactured Products: carpeting, fabric, food products, paints, paper products, pharmaceuticals, transportation equipment, wood products

Natural Resources: crushed stone, granite, kaolin, limestone, sand and gravel, shrimp

Business and Trade: banking, insurance, real estate, tourism, wholesale and retail trade

Peaches

CALENDAR OF CELEBRATIONS

King Week Atlanta honors one of its greatest sons each January. For ten days the city is filled with arts events and speeches commemorating Reverend Martin Luther King Jr.'s struggle for racial equality and harmony.

Augusta Cutting Horse Futurity and Festival Augusta hosts one of the world's top horse events each January. In addition to watching horse competitions at this festival with a western feel, you can also see displays of cowboy equipment and a cattle drive.

Winter Storytelling Festival Tales from around the world are brought to life at this Atlanta festival each January. When not listening to the spellbinding stories, you can watch jugglers or old-fashioned singers perform.

St. Patrick's Day Festival For a week each March everyone in Savannah is Irish at the nation's second-largest celebration of Irishness. A half million people show up for the parade, in which even dogs are dressed in green.

Cherry Blossom Festival The streets of downtown Macon burst into a riot of pink blossoms each March, when the cherry trees bloom. To celebrate, arts and crafts booths, musicians, and festivalgoers fill the streets.

Cherry Blossom Festival

Vidalia Onion Festival Vidalia honors its famously sweet onions at this April event. There's an onion cook-off, an onion-eating contest, and lots of booths selling foods made with Vidalia onions. If you don't like onions, you might still enjoy the air show and the fireworks display.

Brunswick Harborfest Each May Brunswick celebrates its history as a fishing port. Festivalgoers can tour a shrimp boat, see the blessing of the fleet, watch a water parade and powerboat races, and eat lots of shrimp.

Civil War Encampment You can get a feel for what life was like for Civil War soldiers at this July event in Atlanta. Reenactors portraying people from both sides of the conflict tell stories to explain their experiences. Music and food from the time contribute to the Civil War atmosphere.

Civil War Encampment

Southern National Drag Boat Races Billed as the world's richest drag boat races, this popular event is held on the Savannah River in Augusta in July. The boats reach speeds of 250 miles per hour (402 km per hour).

Sea Island Festival The traditional Gullah culture is honored on Saint Simons Island in August. You can eat traditional foods cooked over outdoor fires, learn traditional dances, or watch how fishnets and baskets are woven.

Big Pig Jig You'll eat your fill of barbecue at this celebration of the hog in Vienna each October. More than a hundred teams compete in the barbecue contest, but some people think the snorts and oinks of the hog-calling contest are the most fun.

Mules Day More than 50,000 people show up in the tiny town of Calvary each November to watch mule judging and a mule parade. This old-fashioned event also features a barbecue, a fish fry, a square dance, and syrup-making and tobacco-spitting contests.

Christmas in Savannah Old-time decorations enliven some of Savannah's most beautiful homes during the holiday season. You can tour some of these historic homes and also enjoy caroling and a candlelight tour of the city.

STATE STARS

Kim Basinger (1953–   ) is a popular actress known for her sultry roles. After beginning her career as a model, she broke into film in 1981. She was soon appearing in such movies as *Batman* and *Final Analysis*. Basinger earned her highest acclaim, winning an Academy Award for Best Supporting Actress, for her performance in *L.A. Confidential*. Basinger was born in Athens.

Kim Basinger

Julian Bond (1940–   ), a civil rights leader and politician, was born in Tennessee and attended Morehouse College in Atlanta. He was one of the founders of the Student Nonviolent Coordinating Committee in 1960 and helped it become important in the drive to end segregation. He was elected to the Georgia house of representatives in 1965, but the house refused to let him take his seat because he opposed the Vietnam War. The U.S. Supreme Court eventually ruled that this violated his right to free speech. He was finally seated in 1967. Bond served in the Georgia legislature until 1987.

Julian Bond

James Brown (1928–2006), a native of Macon, was a soul singer whose high-energy shows earned him the nickname the Hardest Working Man in Show Business. Brown began his career in the late 1940s as a gospel singer. By the mid-1950s he was focusing more on rhythm and blues. In 1956 he had his first big hit, "Please, Please, Please." Brown dominated the rhythm-and-blues charts from the mid-1960s through the early 1970s with songs such as "Papa's Got a Brand New Bag" and "I Got You." Brown was one of the first ten inductees into the Rock and Roll Hall of Fame.

Jim Brown (1936–   ), one of the best running backs in football history, led the National Football League in rushing eight times in his nine-year career. As a running back Brown had it all—speed, power, and agility. He was also remarkably sturdy; he never missed a game because of injury. Brown, who spent his entire career with the Cleveland Browns, won the Most Valuable Player award three times and was elected to the Pro Football Hall of Fame in 1971. He was born on Saint Simons Island.

Jim Brown

Asa Griggs Candler (1851–1929) established the Coca-Cola Company in 1892 after purchasing the business from pharmacist John Pemberton, who had developed the drink. Candler marketed Coca-Cola widely, putting it on murals, posters, and drinking glasses. He was also the first person to use coupons to lure customers. Candler quickly made the Coca-Cola Company into one of the most successful businesses in the South. He retired from the company in 1915 and was elected mayor of Atlanta. He was born near Villa Rica.

Jimmy Carter (1924–   ), the thirty-ninth president of the United States, was born in Plains. He worked as a naval officer and a peanut farmer before turning his attention to politics. Carter served in the Georgia senate and as governor before being elected president in 1976. Since leaving office, Carter has helped negotiate during several foreign crises and is widely respected for his charitable works, particularly with Habitat for Humanity, a group that builds homes for needy people.

Ray Charles (1930–2004), born in Albany, was a gifted singer and musician and one of the primary architects of modern soul music. Blind from the disease glaucoma at age seven, Charles played country and western music and jazz before finding his own style, a mixture of blues and gospel music. He recorded "I Got a Woman" in an Atlanta radio station in 1955 and continued to record hit after hit through the 1960s. By the 1980s Charles had become one of the most beloved and admired performers in the nation. He received Grammy's Lifetime Achievement Award in 1987.

Jimmy Carter

Ty Cobb (1886–1961), a native of Narrows, was one of the greatest baseball players of all time. During his long career with the Detroit Tigers, he established several records that still stand, including the highest career batting average, at .366, and the most runs scored, at 2,245. Cobb was famously mean and temperamental, but his talent was undeniable. He led the American League in steals during six seasons and won the league batting title nine years in a row. In 1936 he became one of the first five players elected to the National Baseball Hall of Fame.

Ty Cobb

Oliver Hardy (1892–1957)
was one of the most popular
comedians in film history, as half
of the Laurel and Hardy comedy
duo. The pudgy Hardy and the
thin Stan Laurel first teamed up
in the 1927 short *Duck Soup*.
In the more than one hundred
movies they made, each played
a similar character. Laurel
was always getting them into
trouble, and the situation would
get messier and messier until
Hardy's volcanic temper finally
exploded. Their films, including
Sons of the Desert, *Babes in
Toyland*, and *The Music Box*,
remain favorites today. Hardy
was born in Harlem, Georgia.

Oliver Hardy

Doc Holliday (1851–1887), who was born in Griffin, was a legendary
gambler and gunfighter. He worked as a dentist in the East but moved
west in 1872 because the dry climate was supposed to be better for his
ailing lungs. There, his gunfighting became legendary. In 1881 he was
involved in the famous gunfight at the O.K. Corral.

Charlayne Hunter-Gault (1942–   ) was one of two students who
forced the University of Georgia to open its doors to African

Americans. She was born in South Carolina but moved to Atlanta when she was nine years old. She wanted to be a journalist, and the University of Georgia, which was all white at the time, had the only journalism school in the state. In 1961, she and another black student were admitted to the university. She eventually became a writer for the *New Yorker* and *The New York Times* and a correspondent on television's *McNeil/Lehrer NewsHour*.

Bobby Jones (1902–1971), a native of Atlanta, is considered by some to be the greatest golfer ever. In 1926 he became the first player to win the U.S. and British Opens in the same year. All told, he won the U.S. Open four times, the British Open three times, and the U.S. National Amateur Championship five times. In 1934 he founded the prestigious Masters Golf Tournament.

Martin Luther King Jr. (1929–1968) was the preeminent civil rights leader of the 1950s and 1960s. King, who was born in Atlanta, was a Baptist minister. He first gained national recognition in 1955 for leading a bus boycott in Montgomery, Alabama, in protest over the city's practice of segregated seating on buses. King, who was a powerful and mesmerizing speaker, is perhaps best remembered for his "I Have a Dream" speech, delivered in Washington, D.C., in 1963. King, who advocated nonviolent protest, received the Nobel Peace Prize in 1964. He was assassinated in 1968.

Little Richard (1932–   ) was the wildest of the early rock-and-roll stars, famous for his pounding piano, enthusiastic singing, and occasional screams. His outrageous performances and songs had a strong influence on later groups, such as the Rolling Stones and the Beatles.

Martin Luther King Jr.

In 1956 Little Richard had his first hit with "Tutti Frutti," a song with nonsense lyrics but whose good-natured exuberance has made it a classic. He soon had hit after hit, including "Long Tall Sally" and "Good Golly Miss Molly." In 1986 Little Richard became one of the first performers elected to the Rock and Roll Hall of Fame. He was born in Macon.

Crawford Long (1815–1878) was the doctor credited with performing the first operation using ether as an anesthetic, which was a huge advance in surgery. Ether has a strong smell and causes people to lose consciousness when they inhale it. In 1842 Long gave a patient ether before removing a tumor. Within a few years ether became common in the operating room and remained so for a hundred years. Long was born in Danielsville.

Juliette Gordon Low (1860–1927), a native of Savannah, founded the Girl Scouts of America. Low was a friend of Robert Baden-Powell, who founded the Boy Scouts. Low organized a troop of Girl Scouts in Savannah in 1912. She served as the president of the Girl Scouts of America until 1920.

Juliette Gordon Low

Carson McCullers (1917–1967), who was born in Columbus, wrote novels that drew on her southern childhood. Her books, which are usually set in small towns, are filled with lonely characters. Her most famous novels include *The Heart Is a Lonely Hunter* and *The Member of the Wedding*.

Willie McTell (1901–1959), one of the greatest of all blues singers and guitarists, was renowned for his guitar mastery and warm voice. McTell, who was born blind, began playing harmonica and accordion as a child. He eventually switched to guitar and earned acclaim for the delicacy and agility with which he played the twelve-string. He began recording in 1927 and soon laid down some of his most famous songs, including "Statesboro Blues." McTell was born in Thomson.

Willie McTell

Johnny Mercer (1909–1976) was a songwriter, most famous for writing the lyrics for many hit songs in movies and on the pop record charts. He wrote the words to such classics as "I'm an Old Cowhand" and "Jeepers

Creepers." Over his long career he won three Academy Awards, including one for "Moon River" from the film *Breakfast at Tiffany's*. Mercer was a native of Savannah.

Jessye Norman (1945–   ) is an opera singer, famous around the world for her rich, emotional voice and commanding stage presence. Norman, who was born in Augusta, first gained recognition when she won a voice competition in Germany in 1968. She made her operatic debut the following year and was soon filling opera houses across the globe. Today she has a reputation as one of the world's most versatile and knowledgeable opera singers.

Flannery O'Connor (1925–1964) was an acclaimed fiction writer whose novels and stories typically have dark humor and grotesque characters. Her work, such as the novel *Wise Blood* and the short story collection *A Good Man Is Hard to Find*, are also strongly influenced by O'Connor's Roman Catholicism. In the last decade of her life O'Connor suffered from lupus, a crippling disease that kept her in bed most of the time at her home in Milledgeville.

Ma Rainey (1867–1939), who was known as the Mother of the Blues, had a powerful, brooding singing style that influenced many younger performers. By the time she cut her first record, in 1923, Rainey was already one of the world's most famous blues singers and had been performing in front of audiences for more than twenty years. She made such songs as "C.C. Rider" and "Bo Weevil Blues" into classics. Rainey was born in Columbus.

Jessye Norman

Otis Redding (1941–1967), a singer known for his grainy voice and emotional ballads, was born in Macon. Redding began recording in 1960 and soon had such hits as "Try a Little Tenderness" and "Mr. Pitiful." His most famous song, "(Sittin' on) The Dock of the Bay," was released after he died in a plane crash. It earned him two Grammy Awards and was his only song to hit number one on the pop charts.

Otis Redding

Jackie Robinson (1919–1972) broke the color barrier in Major League Baseball. Robinson was a remarkable all-around athlete. At the University of California at Los Angeles he became the first student .to earn varsity letters in four sports: football, basketball, baseball, and track. When Robinson began playing professional baseball, the Major Leagues did not allow black players. So instead, he played with the Kansas City Monarchs in the Negro Leagues. In 1947 he joined the Brooklyn Dodgers, becoming the first black player in the majors. His aggressive baserunning and graceful fielding helped the Dodgers win the National League pennant, and he was named Rookie of the Year. In 1962 he became the first African-American player inducted into the National Baseball Hall of Fame. Robinson was born in Cairo.

Sequoya (1767?–1843) invented the Cherokee alphabet. Born in Tennessee, Sequoya later settled in Cherokee County, Georgia, where he worked as a silversmith and trader. In an effort to preserve Cherokee culture, he developed an alphabet consisting of eighty-six characters, which represented every syllable in the Cherokee language. Soon books and newspapers were being published in Cherokee.

Sequoya

Clarence Thomas (1948–   ) is the second African American to serve on the U.S. Supreme Court. Thomas began his career as an assistant attorney general for Missouri. While serving as the chairman of the Equal Employment Opportunity Commission, he became known for his conservative beliefs. Thomas, who was appointed to the Court in 1991, was born in Savannah.

Ted Turner (1938–   ) is one of the most famous and successful businesspeople in America. Turner, who was born in Ohio, got his start when he took over his family's billboard business in 1963. In 1970 he bought a television station in Atlanta, which he eventually turned into WTBS, the first "superstation," which used satellites to send programming to cable systems around the country. This innovation fostered the spread of cable television. In 1980 Turner founded Cable News Network (CNN), the first twenty-four-hour all-news television station. At the time Turner also owned the Atlanta Braves baseball team, the Atlanta Hawks basketball team, and the Atlanta Thrashers hockey team. In 1997 he made headlines when he pledged $1 billion to the United Nations, one of the largest charitable donations in history.

Alice Walker (1944–   ) writes books about the hardships faced by black women, particularly in earlier times. Her best-known work, the novel *The Color Purple*, was published in 1982 and won a Pulitzer Prize and an American Book Award. More recently, she has published *In Search of Our Mothers' Gardens*, a collection of essays and speeches about her experience as a black woman in America. Walker was born in Eatonton.

Ted Turner

Chattooga Wild and Scenic River (Clayton) Float down a river through spectacular gorges filled with lush scenery, rocky outcrops, and refreshing waterfalls.

New Echota State Historic Site (Calhoun) In 1825 the Cherokee Nation established a capital at New Echota. Today you can visit the old council house, which has been restored, along with the courthouse and a store made from logs from the 1830s. The site also includes the shop where the first Cherokee newspaper, the *Cherokee Phoenix*, was printed in 1828.

Chattooga Wild and Scenic River

Callaway Gardens

Callaway Gardens (Pine Mountain) Hike down trails past luxurious
flowering plants, enter a glass conservatory where a thousand
butterflies flutter around your head, and let your imagination run wild
at the topiary garden, where plants are cut into fanciful shapes, such as
the Mad Hatter.

Paradise Gardens (Summerville) Folk artist Howard Finster created this
unique garden filled with sculptures made of aluminum foil and old
bicycle parts.

Brasstown Bald (Helen) Climb a steep trail to the top of Georgia's
highest peak for a spectacular view in every direction. You can see
four states from the summit.

Brasstown Bald

National Science Center's Fort Discovery (Augusta) At this high-tech museum you can feel what it's like to walk on the moon and then explore nearly three hundred other interactive exhibits.

Dahlonega Gold Museum (Dahlonega) This museum is housed in the oldest public building in northern Georgia. Inside you'll see exhibits of gold coins, nuggets, and mining tools, along with displays about Appalachian culture.

Dahlonega Gold Museum

Amicalola Falls State Park (Dahlonega) At this park you can admire fabulous falls that drop 729 feet (222 m) and wondrous views of the Blue Ridge Mountains.

Cloudland Canyon State Park (Trenton) Lovers of the outdoors won't want to miss the hike through thick forests, past dramatic waterfalls, and up to a point with an extraordinary view in one of Georgia's most scenic areas.

High Museum of Art (Atlanta) This eye-catching building contains four stories of art, from ancient pottery to contemporary paintings.

Atlanta History Center (Atlanta) In the history museum you can learn about the civil rights movement and southern culture. But the center also includes a grand early-twentieth-century house with elaborate gardens and a working farm built in the style of the 1840s, in which reenacters perform tasks such as sheep shearing and weaving.

Martin Luther King Jr. National Historic site (Atlanta) This site includes King's birthplace, the Ebenezer Baptist Church, where he was a pastor in the 1960s, and his gravesite.

Soul Food Museum (Atlanta) This unique museum and store features food and other products developed and marketed by African Americans.

Stone Mountain (Stone Mountain) The largest relief sculpture in the world depicts the Confederate heroes Jefferson Davis, Robert E. Lee, and Stonewall Jackson.

Cloudland Canyon State Park

Franklin Delano Roosevelt Little White House State Historic Site and Roosevelt Memorial Museum (Warm Springs) The house looks much as it did when President Roosevelt lived there. The museum contains many of the president's personal belongings.

Ocmulgee National Monument (Macon) At this site you can see exhibits and artifacts detailing 12,000 years of Indian settlement. Trails lead visitors around nine ceremonial mounds built by Indians, including the Great Temple Mound, which is more than 40 feet (12 m) high. You can also see a restored earth lodge that would have been a typical meeting place.

Georgia Music Hall of Fame (Macon) You'll see and hear all about Georgia's varied musicians, from James Brown to Johnny Mercer, at this museum. It even has areas designed to look like a jazz club, a church, and a rock-and-roll record store, so you can get a feel for where the music came from.

Andersonville National Historic Site (Andersonville) This Confederate military prison was built to house ten thousand prisoners but held as many as 33,000. On a visit to the prison you can see the escape tunnels prisoners dug and diaries and photographs that bring the prisoners' stories to life. More than 17,000 Union soldiers are buried at the Andersonville National Cemetery.

Davenport House (Savannah) The movement to save Savannah's famous buildings began in the 1950s, when a group of citizens got together to preserve this lovely house, built in 1820. Today you can tour the home, which is filled with antiques.

Davenport House

Saint Simons Lighthouse

Okefenokee Swamp (Folkston) The dark brown waters and islands in this sprawling swamp are home to lots of animals, including alligators and black bears. A walk along boardwalks, past cypress trees covered in moss, will take you through this unusual landscape.

Saint Simons Lighthouse (Saint Simons Island) Climb to the top of this 104-foot (32-m) lighthouse for a wonderful view. The light has been in operation since 1872.

Cumberland Island National Seashore (Saint Marys) Only three hundred visitors a day are allowed into this preserve so that the island will remain pristine and able to support the loggerhead turtles, bobcats, and wild horses that live there.

FUN FACTS

Each year Georgia produces 1.1 billion square yards of carpeting. That is enough to wrap a 12-foot-wide (4-m-wide) strip of carpet around the Earth four times.

The first golf course in the United States was laid out in Savannah in 1794.

The Cyclorama Building in Atlanta contains the largest mural in the world. This painting, which is 358 feet (109 m) long, shows the Battle of Atlanta during the Civil War.

FIND OUT MORE

Want to know more about Georgia? Check the library or bookstore for these titles.

GENERAL STATE BOOKS

Crutchfield, James A. *It Happened in Georgia*. Guilford, CT: TwoDot, 2007.

Sceurman, Mark and Mark Moran. *Weird Georgia*. New York: Sterling, 2006.

SPECIAL INTEREST BOOKS

Doak, Robin. *Voices from Colonial America: Georgia 1521–1776*. Des Moines, IA: National Geographic Children's Books, 2006.

Fleming, Alice. *Martin Luther King, Jr.: A Dream of Hope*. New York: Sterling, 2008.

Perdue, Theda. *The Cherokees (Indians of North America)*. New York: Chelsea House, 2004.

Ryan, Bernard Jr. *Jimmy Carter: U.S. President and Humanitarian*. New York: Ferguson Publishing Company, 2006.

Sonnerborn, Liz. *A Primary Source History of the Colony of Georgia.* New York: Rosen Central, 2005.

Wiener, Roberts and James R. Arnold. *Georgia: The History of Georgia Colony, 1732–1776.* Chicago, IL: Raintree, 2004.

Wiggins, David N. *Remembering Georgia's Confederates (Images of America).* San Francisco, CA: Arcadia Publishing, 2005.

FICTION

Sullivan, E. J., author; Christena Brooks, illustrator. *The Georgia Night Before Christmas.* Raleigh, NC: Sweetwater Press, 2005.

VIDEOS

Atlanta Cyclorama, Experience the Battle of Atlanta. 35 min., Finley-Holiday Film Corp.

Atlanta's Olympic Glory. 210 min., PBS Home Video.

WEBSITES

GeorgiaInfo
http://georgiainfo.galileo.usg.edu
This is the largest and most comprehensive website containing information on the state.

Georgia in the Civil War

www.cherokeerose.com

This website about Georgia history includes photographs, maps, and links.

State of Georgia Home Page

www.georgia.gov

This site provides information and links on education, business, government, and other topics.

Index

Page numbers in **boldface** are illustrations and charts.

ABOUT THE AUTHOR

Steve Otfinoski has written more than 130 books for children and young adults, including Marshall Cavendish's twelve-volume transportation series Here We Go! He is also the author of *New Hampshire* in the Celebrate the States series.